DATE DUE

DEMCO 128-8155

African American Literature.

Lucent Library of Black History

Stephen Currie

LUCENT BOOKS
A part of Gale, Cengage Learning

GALE
CENGAGE Learning

Detroit • New York • San Francisco • New Haven, Conn • Waterville, Maine • London

810.9
CUR

GALE
CENGAGE Learning

LIBRARY OF CONGRESS CATALOGING-IN-PUBLICATION DATA

Currie, Stephen, 1960-
  African American literature / by Stephen Currie.
      p. cm. -- (Lucent library of Black history)
  Includes bibliographical references and index.
  ISBN 978-1-4205-0383-8 (hardcover)
  1. African Americans--History--Juvenile literature. 2. American literature--African American authors--History and criticism--Juvenile literature. 3. African Americans--Intellectual life--Juvenile literature. 4. African Americans in literature--Juvenile literature. I. Title.
  E185.C977 2011
  810.9'896073--dc22
                                                                2011003923

Lucent Books
27500 Drake Rd.
Farmington Hills, MI 48331

ISBN-13: 978-1-4205-0383-8
ISBN-10: 1-4205-0383-9

Printed in the United States of America
2 3 4 5 6 7 15 14 13 12

Contents

Foreword 4

Introduction
African American Literature Through the Years 6

Chapter One
The Oral Tradition and the First Black
Writers: 1600–1800 9

Chapter Two
Slave and Free: 1800–1865 22

Chapter Three
After the Civil War: 1865–1918 37

Chapter Four
The Harlem Renaissance: 1918–1940 52

Chapter Five
Through the Civil Rights Struggle: 1940–1969 68

Chapter Six
Into a New Century: 1970–Present 83

Notes 98
Glossary 102
For More Information 103
Index 105
Picture Credits 111
About the Author 112

Foreword

It has been more than 500 years since Africans were first brought to the New World in shackles, and over 140 years since slavery was formally abolished in the United States. Over 50 years have passed since the fallacy of "separate but equal" was obliterated in the American courts, and some 40 years since the watershed Civil Rights Act of 1964 guaranteed the rights and liberties of all Americans, especially those of color. Over time, these changes have become celebrated landmarks in American history. In the twenty-first century, African American men and women are politicians, judges, diplomats, professors, deans, doctors, artists, athletes, business owners, and home owners. For many, the scars of the past have melted away in the opportunities that have been found in contemporary society. Observers such as Peter N. Kirsanow, who sits on the U.S. Commission of Civil Rights, point to these accomplishments and conclude, "The growing black middle class may be viewed as proof that most of the civil rights battles have been won."

In spite of these legal victories, however, prejudice and inequality have persisted in American society. In 2003, African Americans comprised just 12 percent of the nation's population, yet accounted for 44 percent of its prison inmates and 24 percent of its poor. Racially motivated hate crimes continue to appear on the pages of major newspapers in many American cities. Furthermore, many African Americans still experience either overt or muted racism in their daily lives. A 1996 study undertaken by Professor Nancy Krieger of the Harvard School of Public Health, for example, found that 80 percent of the African American participants reported having experienced racial discrimination in one or more settings, including at work or school, applying for housing and medical care, from the police or in the courts, and on the street or in a public setting.

It is for these reasons that many believe the struggle for racial equality and justice is far from over. These episodes of discrimination threaten to shatter the illusion that America has completely overcome its racist past, causing many black Americans to become increasingly frustrated and confused. Scholar and writer Ellis Cose has described this splintered state in the following way: "I have done everything I was supposed to do. I have stayed out of trouble with the law, gone to the right schools, and worked myself nearly to death. What more do they want? Why in God's name won't they accept me as a full human being?" For Cose and others, the struggle for equality and justice has yet to be fully achieved.

In many subtle yet important ways the traumatic experiences of slavery and segregation continue to inform the way race is discussed and experienced in the twenty-first century. Indeed, it is possible that America will always grapple with the fallout from its distressing past. Ulric Haynes, dean of the Hofstra University School of Business has said, "Perhaps race will always matter, given the historical circumstances under which we came to this country." But studying this past and understanding how it contributes to present-day dialogues about race and history in America is a critical component of contemporary education. To this end, the Lucent Library of Black History offers a thorough look at the experiences that have shaped the black community and the American people as a whole. Annotated bibliographies provide readers with ideas for further research, while fully documented primary and secondary source quotations enhance the text. Each book in the series explores a different episode of black history; together they provide students with a wealth of information as well as launching points for further study and discussion.

Introduction

African American Literature Through the Years

Today, African American authors are very much in the mainstream of American literature. It is easy to find the novels and poetry of modern-day black writers such as Maya Angelou, Walter Mosley, and Alice Walker in libraries, bookstores, and online catalogs throughout the United States. Even the writings of earlier African Americans are readily available. The novels of early-twentieth-century author Zora Neale Hurston, the memoirs of orator and former slave Frederick Douglass, and the nonfiction of black leader W.E.B. DuBois, just to name a few, are widely read by both black and white Americans.

These works are not merely accessible, they are also taken seriously by American critics and scholars. Colleges and universities today offer courses and concentrations in the literature of African America, and critics routinely include works such as Richard Wright's memoir *Black Boy*, Langston Hughes's poem "Harlem," and Toni Morrison's novel *Beloved* on lists of the greatest American works of literature. By all standards, African American writers today are well respected, and the best of their works are extremely popular with critics as well as with the general public.

It was not always this way, however. Only in relatively recent times have black authors received much attention at all. This lack of recognition is related to the long-standing white prejudice in America against people of African descent. Through much of American history black Americans have been abused, ignored, and even enslaved; kept from fully participating in society; and offered substandard education—if indeed any education at all.

Moreover, for many years white Americans typically believed that blacks were inferior to whites, both morally and intellectually, and that no person of African background could possibly have anything interesting to say. Indeed, when a young African American woman named Phillis Wheatley published several poems in the late 1700s, a group of influential white men from New England openly doubted that Wheatley, as a black person, could actually have been the author.

The years from Phillis Wheatley to Maya Angelou, from colonial America to the present day, have seen dramatic changes in African American literature and how it has been received by readers

African American poet Phillis Wheatley published this book of poetry in 1773. Many white people thought she could not have written it because she was black.

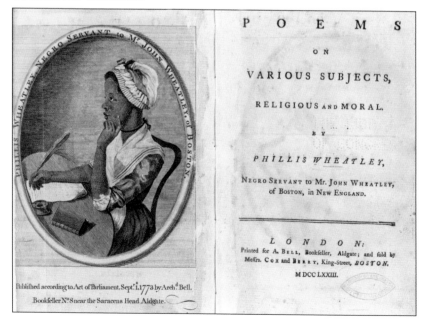

of all races. Little by little the works of black authors have crept into the consciousness of Americans, and little by little Americans both black and white have come to accept and appreciate these works. Scorn for the notion that any black person could actually write a poem or a novel, an attitude common among Americans for many years, has disappeared completely as black writers of today routinely win awards, receive critical acclaim, and enjoy widespread popularity. It has been a long journey; but African American literature has successfully traveled this distance.

Part of the reason for the change is the fact that blacks as a group have made important gains in society since the founding of the United States. Early notions of black inferiority have largely vanished as African Americans have entered politics, business, and the arts. Given education and a more tolerant racial climate, blacks have demonstrated their abilities in dozens of fields. It seems ludicrous to think that anyone today would question whether Alice Walker could have truly written her critically acclaimed *The Color Purple* or whether Edward P. Jones was the actual author of the prize-winning novel *The Known World*.

But another factor has been perhaps as important in establishing black literature as a vital force in the United States today. That factor is the quality of African American poetry, essays, fiction, and drama over the years. Some of the most-praised American writing of the past two centuries has been produced by African Americans—the novels of Ralph Ellison, the poetry of Gwendolyn Brooks, the essays of James Weldon Johnson. Rooted in black history and steeped in African American culture, the works of black Americans through time have not only been remarkable literary works but have revealed much about the unique culture that produced them. Americans' increasing tolerance for racial differences has certainly helped African American literature to shine, but much of the credit goes to the quality of the works themselves. Their richness and brilliance have made African American writings impossible to ignore.

Chapter One

The Oral Tradition and the First Black Writers: 1600–1800

Beginning in the early 1500s and continuing for over three hundred years, European merchants and sailors brought a steady stream of captives from Africa to the New World. Once arriving in the Americas, the Africans were sold into slavery. As slaves, they were forced to labor without pay, frequently working six days a week from dawn till after dusk. Most were beaten and whipped for the slightest hint of disobedience—and sometimes for no reason at all. Nearly all were kept illiterate and ignorant of the world around them. Over the years, thousands upon thousands of slaves came to North America. By 1860 about 4 million slaves lived in the United States.

During these years, not all Americans of African descent were slaves. Some were free: Legally, they belonged to no one and could work for themselves. In reality, though, the lives of most free blacks were not much better than the lives of the slaves. Few were skilled laborers. Fewer still could read. Most lived in poverty, and virtually all faced racial prejudice at every turn. Laws and customs barred free African Americans from certain professions and often kept them from living in certain communities or sections of larger towns. Nor did free African Americans account for much of the total black population. In 1860, only about half a million American blacks were free, or about 11 percent of the total.

Circumstances such as near-constant labor, extreme poverty, and an almost complete lack of education were powerful barriers to the creation of great literature. But even in these difficult times, African Americans maintained a literary tradition. Both orally and in writing, free blacks and slaves created stories, poems, and other works and handed them down from one generation to the next. The literature of these early years reflected the experiences of black Americans and helped them make sense of their world.

From these beginnings, African American literature would move ever closer to the mainstream of American writing. In the years to come, generations of black writers would experiment with

African Americans brought with them from West Africa a rich tradition of stories, poems, and songs. They spread these stories through storytellers and singers.

new forms and new genres, write on topics never before dreamed of by black slaves of the colonial period, and discuss with force and eloquence what it meant—and what it still means—to be black in a society dominated by whites. These writers would earn ever greater acceptance by their fellow Americans, both white and black, and many of them would have an impact on the nation's politics and history. These triumphs were possible only because of the pioneering efforts of the men and women of the 1600s and 1700s who helped to build the foundation of black literature in the America to come.

Oral Tradition

Nearly all the African slaves in the Americas came from preliterate societies—that is, from peoples who did not read and write. The lack of a written language did not imply, however, that these societies lacked literature. On the contrary, West African cultures had a rich and vibrant tradition of stories, poems, and songs. They spread these works through the spoken word: by means of storytellers and singers, for example, rather than through written texts. Historians and other experts use the term *oral tradition* to describe this way of passing stories from one generation to the next.

The first Africans in the New World brought their oral traditions with them. The stories they told were the stories popular among the West African peoples they belonged to. Their poetry had been created by fellow West Africans over the course of many years. These stories and songs offered hope and comfort to the newcomers. Though they had been taken from their homes and families, they could at least hold fast to the literary traditions of their peoples. Indeed, the early slaves told these stories and sang these songs frequently. As one folklorist puts it, "The elements of storytelling were included in the only 'baggage' [the slaves] could carry with them: their traditional styles [and] their ways of performing and celebrating."[1]

Over time the connections between black Americans and their African origins began to fade. Christianity supplanted tribal religions; African languages were replaced by English. The songs and stories of West Africa were living traditions, however, interpreted in different ways by different storytellers and singers, and as the lives of the new African Americans changed, their oral literature

Benjamin Banneker

Benjamin Banneker was a free black who lived most of his life in Maryland. Fascinated by science, mathematics, and engineering, Banneker built what may have been the first clock produced in the United States. He also helped plan the layout of Washington, D.C., and wrote almanacs detailing his knowledge of astronomy.

In 1791 Banneker wrote a famous letter to Thomas Jefferson, then serving as George Washington's secretary of state. Like most white Americans of his time, Jefferson believed that blacks were much less intelligent than whites. Banneker's letter sought to prove Jefferson wrong. He argued that blacks and whites were much more alike than they were different. "One universal Father hath given Being to us all," Banneker pointed out. "However variable we may be in science or religion, however diversified in situation [social and economic class] or colour, we are all of the same family." The lowly position of blacks in America, Banneker asserted, had nothing to do with innate ability and everything to do with racism and slavery.

In case Jefferson did not find this argument compelling, Banneker also enclosed one of his almanacs. He hoped that upon seeing the book, Jefferson would be impressed with Banneker's insight and intelligence and would rethink his position. Jefferson was indeed intrigued with Banneker's almanac and cogent argument; but Banneker's letter is remembered today less for the impression that it made on Jefferson than for the clear thinking it demonstrated on the subject of race.

Quoted in Richard Barksdale and Keneth Kinnamon, ed. *Black Writers of America: A Comprehensive Anthology.* New York: Macmillan, 1972.

Benjamin Banneker was fascinated with science, mathematics, and engineering. He may have built the first clock produced in the United States.

changed accordingly. By the early 1800s the folklore of black Americans remained related to the traditional songs and stories of West Africa, but it had become something new: a body of literary work uniquely rooted in the black American experience.

Stories

The stories of early African Americans took on a variety of forms. Some of the best known today are a series of animal folktales that focus on a character called Br'er Rabbit. Br'er Rabbit is a trickster—a sly creature who relies on his wits to escape his more powerful enemy, Br'er Fox. Though other characters populate the dozens of Br'er Rabbit tales recorded by nineteenth-century folklorists, Br'er Rabbit is the hero of most of these stories. The central theme of many of them is Br'er Rabbit's ability to outwit the fox.

In one famous story, for instance, Br'er Fox has captured the little rabbit and is wondering how best to torment him. Br'er Rabbit, seemingly alarmed, begs his enemy not to throw him into the briar patch, a nearby tangle of weeds and thorns. "Roas[t] me, Br'er Fox," pleads the rabbit. "Snatch out my eyeballs [and] cut off my legs . . . but don't fling me in dat brier-patch." Convinced that Br'er Rabbit's distress is genuine, Br'er Fox promptly tosses his enemy into the brier-patch. He regrets it, though, when he hears Br'er Rabbit scampering happily away. "Bred en bawn [born] in a brier-patch, Br'er Fox," the rabbit calls out, "bred en bawn in a brier-patch!"[2]

Another series of stories told by African Americans before the Civil War involves a fictional slave, usually known as John. Most of these stories describe John's attempts to fool his master or to gain his freedom. In one story, for example, John claims to be in direct contact with God. He arranges for a friend to climb to the top of a tree, carrying a variety of items with him. While his master watches, John then calls for the items in turn. The master is shocked to see each item fall from the tree. Believing that John really is giving orders to God, the rather dimwitted master sets John free and gives him "forty acres an' uh thousand dollars"[3] as well.

These stories, like most other black folktales, powerfully reflect the realities of life in slavery. The John tales, for instance, sprang directly from the experiences of slaves with harsh and often unpredictable masters. Similarly, slaves often identified with Br'er

Some of the best-known early African American folktales are those of
the wily Br'er Rabbit.

Rabbit, who despite his physical disadvantages often prevailed against Br'er Fox. The rabbit's victories over his enemy gave the slaves hope that they too might overcome their own disadvantages. Though the slave owners were richer, better educated, and better armed than the slaves, the Br'er Rabbit stories seemed to say, they were not necessarily more intelligent—and might not always come out on top.

Songs

Song lyrics represented another important part of the West African oral tradition. As with stories, the songs of nineteenth-century African Americans were not the same as those of West Africans of previous generations. The realities of the black experience in America led to songs with very different themes and topics from the songs native to West Africa. Just as the stories of the black oral tradition formed part of the foundation for African American literature, so too did the songs.

Many of the earliest songs sung by African Americans were work songs. It was common for black laborers to sing as they performed their jobs, especially when groups of workers were carrying out a repetitive task such as harvesting crops or pounding in fence posts. Other songs were funny and lighthearted. "I kep' a walking and they kep' a talking," reads a line from a pre–Civil War song known as "Charleston Gals"; "I danced with a gal with a hole in her stocking."[4]

By far the best-known African American folk songs of the time, though, are religious songs called spirituals. The spirituals, which date to the mid-1700s if not earlier, expressed the Christian faith of African American slaves. Some of the spirituals were joyous; they celebrated the expected triumph of Jesus over evil and waited for the day when the singer would be taken up to heaven. "O blow your trumpet, Gabriel," ran a song of this type, referencing a traditional Christian belief that the angel Gabriel would announce the end of the world with a blast of a trumpet.

Blow your trumpet louder

And I want dat trumpet to blow me home

To my new Jerusalem.[5]

Though the Christian message of salvation was a powerful one for black Americans, not all spirituals were joyful. On the contrary, many were introspective, even sad. These were known as "sorrow songs." Meant to be sung slowly and softly, sorrow songs mourned the trials of life on earth and called on God and Jesus for emotional support. "Sometimes I feel like a motherless child," runs the text of one sorrow song, "a long way from home."[6]

A third type of spiritual simply retold stories from the Bible. Most related stories from the Old Testament, such as the narrative of Adam and Eve or the visions of the prophet Ezekiel. The tale of the Exodus was a particularly common subject for spirituals. This story tells how Moses led the Hebrew people out of slavery in Egypt toward the Promised Land. For the blacks of the American South, the similarities between the Hebrews and their own lives were obvious. The chorus to one famous spiritual about the Exodus runs as follows:

Some of the earliest songs sung by African Americans were work songs.

Go down, Moses,

Way down in Egypt land

Tell ole Pharaoh

Let my people go.[7]

Like the stories and the work songs of the African American oral tradition, spirituals were among the first examples of black literature in the United States. Even today, they remain among the best known of all art forms created by black Americans. They are widely admired for their imagery and their ability to touch listeners and readers two or more centuries after their creation. Indeed, the themes and ideas in the words of spirituals continue to influence current African American literature.

Early Writers

The bulk of early African American literature was spoken or sung, not written, and given the low levels of literacy among blacks of the time this should come as no surprise. Nevertheless, a few black writers of the late 1700s and early 1800s did manage to get their work published. One of the first was a man named Jupiter Hammon. Born in New York in 1711, Hammon lived his whole life as a slave. His owners, however, allowed him considerable independence from an early age. Unlike almost all other slaves of the 1700s, for instance, Hammon went to school and learned to read and write. Later, he became a preacher who spoke often to slave congregations; and he may even have kept the accounts for his owners' business.

In addition to these talents, Hammon was also a poet. In 1761 he became perhaps the first African American to publish a piece of writing—a long religious poem called "An Evening Thought." The verses reflect Hammon's deep faith and his certainty that Jesus will offer salvation to all Christians. "Salvation comes by Jesus Christ alone," Hammon wrote at the start of his poem,

The only Son of God;

Redemption now to every one

That love his holy Word.[8]

Over the next few decades, Hammon went on to publish several more works, including both poetry and prose. Hammon's best-known piece of writing today is a speech he gave in 1786, which he published in pamphlet form a year later. The speech is known as *Address to the Negroes of the State of New York* but is often called simply Hammon's Address. In this speech Hammon, by now well into his seventies, urged his younger black listeners to put Christianity at the center of their lives. "Those of you who can read," he told his audience, "I must beg you to read the Bible." As for those who could not read, he continued, "get those who can read to teach you; but remember that what you learn to read for is to read the Bible."[9]

In his speech, however, Hammon did not focus entirely on religion. He also wrote of slavery and what it meant to be a slave. Living as he did in a world made by and for white people, Hammon was cautious in his statements about slavery. He claimed that he had no desire for freedom and stressed the responsibilities of being a slave. Still, Hammon left no doubt that he disapproved of slavery. "I should be glad," he asserted, "if others, especially the young negroes[,] were to be free."[10]

Phillis Wheatley

Though Hammon was most likely the first African American to publish his writing, he was not the best-known black writer of his time. That honor goes to a poet named Phillis Wheatley. Born about 1753 in present-day Senegal, West Africa, Wheatley was brought to Massachusetts as a girl and sold into slavery. She quickly learned English and impressed her owners with her intelligence and curiosity. They soon taught her to read and write and gave her a solid grounding in the Bible as well.

Wheatley began writing poetry as an adolescent. When she was about seventeen she published her first poem, a reflection on the death of a well-known minister, and followed it with other works in the next several years. Though Wheatley's writing style has gone out of favor since her time, it was very much in keeping with literary trends of the era. Her poems were marked by metaphors, classical references, and formal, high-flown language. A patriotic poem she wrote dating from 1775, for instance, begins with the line "Celestial choir! enthroned in realms of light."[11]

Phillis Wheatley

Phillis Wheatley was able to overcome many barriers in her quest to become a published poet. Her race, however, was certainly a handicap. A Boston publisher refused to print her book simply because she was black. Other whites insisted that people of African descent were unable to write poetry at all, let alone construct the sophisticated stanzas Wheatley produced. In 1772, in fact, a committee of influential Bostonians convened to determine whether Wheatley was really the author of the poems she had published. The committee eventually ruled that the poems were indeed hers, but the fact that the question came up at all indicates the willingness of American whites of the time to downgrade the intelligence and achievements of black people.

Though Wheatley was freed as a young woman, she did not have much opportunity to enjoy her freedom. Her later life was marked by tragedy. She married, but she and her husband had difficulty finding work and lived in poverty for most of their marriage; she had several children, none of whom survived infancy. Wheatley's health was never good, and in 1784 she died, probably not much older than thirty.

The Phillis Wheatley statue at the Boston Women's Memorial. She overcame many barriers to be published but died in poverty.

The themes of Wheatley's poems were typical of her era, too. Poets of the period often wrote about abstract topics, for example, and Wheatley was no exception. She entitled one poem "On Virtue," and her work included verses about ideals such as wisdom, devotion, and education. As with her writing style, Wheatley's themes are no longer fashionable. The combination can make it difficult for modern readers to appreciate Wheatley's work; indeed, the editors of one recent anthology of black literature note that much of her poetry comes across today as "pious sentimentalizing about Truth, Salvation, Mercy, and Goodness."[12]

Still, though tastes have changed, Wheatley's poetry was quite popular in her time. George Washington read and enjoyed at least one of her works, and a book of her poems sold quite well in both England and the colonies. It surely helped Wheatley's reputation that her choice of topics was mainstream and inoffensive. Her poems seldom mentioned slavery or race, which allowed whites to enjoy her work without having to confront difficult moral and political issues. In fact, one of the few poems that discusses Wheatley's race actually describes her gratitude at being removed from Africa:

'Twas mercy brought me from my pagan land,

Taught my benighted soul to understand

That there's a God, that there's a Saviour too;

Once I redemption neither sought nor knew.[13]

Lucy Terry Prince

Hammon and Wheatley were the best-known black writers of their time, but they were not the only ones. According to many sources, for instance, a Massachusetts woman named Lucy Terry Prince composed a poem called "Bars Fight" in 1746. The poem describes a surprise attack by Native Americans on a Massachusetts settlement known as the "Bars," leading to the deaths of several settlers. "Bars Fight" consists of rhyming couplets that detail the grim fates of the colonists. "Oliver Amsden, he was slain," runs a typical line, "which caused his friends much grief and pain."[14]

At this point it is impossible to tell how much of "Bars Fight," if indeed any, was original to Prince. She never published the poem, and may never have written it down. For many decades, the poem circulated only as part of the settlers' oral tradition. Even if Prince wrote a poem about the fight, then, the transcription may not represent her original work. Nonetheless, there is some evidence that Prince did compose a poem about the fight, and as a result several historians credit her as being the first African American poet.

From a stylistic point of view, the works of Hammon, Prince, and other early black writers may not have been impressive. Neither were their insights always compelling. As twentieth-century black writer and critic Arna Bontemps delicately puts it, these earliest writers were followed by others "who had more to say and said it more effectively."[15] Still, when their work is viewed alongside the rich oral tradition that developed among black Americans in the 1700s and beyond, it is clear that these early writers established a foundation for African American literature. The writers who came later owe much to the imagery of the early spirituals, the biting humor of the Br'er Rabbit stories, and the courage and talent of the Hammons, Wheatleys, and Princes who preceded them.

Chapter Two

Slave and Free: 1800–1865

For African Americans, the 1800s began much as the 1700s had ended: with the vast majority of their people living and working in slavery. If anything, though, the blacks of the early 1800s were worse off than the previous generation had been. Though most Northern states had taken steps to abolish, or eliminate, slavery by the early 1800s, the institution was becoming ever more entrenched in the South. A new machine called the cotton gin had made cotton production more profitable than ever before, leading to a rise in demand for slaves. And while earlier Southern leaders, such as Thomas Jefferson and George Washington, had spoken frequently of a desire to see slavery end, the newer ranks of Southern politicians did not share these feelings. To them, slavery presented no moral issues. It was a positive institution, justified by both science and religion, and advocates had no interest in eliminating the system.

The focus of black writers in the first half of the 1800s, not surprisingly, was on slavery. Most of the works produced by African American authors during this period dealt in some way with slaves and the slave system. Some of these writers, born into freedom in the North, attacked slavery in their writings. They used logic, morality, and the force of words to advocate abolitionism in the South. Other authors had once been slaves themselves. They wrote detailed descriptions of the brutalities of the system, based (at least in theory) on their personal experiences. Together the two groups made an important and lasting contribution to African American literature.

Antislavery Writings

One of the first black writers to attack slavery was a man named David Walker, born in North Carolina in 1785. In 1829, soon after moving to Boston, he published *An Appeal to the Coloured Citizens of the World*. Better known today simply as Walker's Appeal, the book was a bitter indictment of slavery. Because Walker had been free from birth, he had never experienced slavery directly. Nonetheless, Walker had spent much of his life in the South. As a result, his understanding of slavery was genuine—and thorough. "I do not speak from hearsay," Walker assured his readers. "What I have written, is what I have seen and heard myself."[16]

What set Walker's Appeal apart from other antislavery writings was not so much Walker's knowledge of slavery, however, but his passion. The book is filled with emotional appeals for blacks of all backgrounds to join in condemning slavery—and stopping it if at all possible. Walker made liberal use of italics and exclamation marks in his book to emphasize his statements. Indeed, he frequently inserted multiple exclamation points at the end of his sentences. "I tell you Americans!" he warned at one point in his book, "that unless you speedily alter your course [by abolishing slavery], *you* and your *Country are gone*!!!!!"[17]

Minister and author Henry Highland Garnet was another black man who wrote frequently about abolition. Unlike Walker, Garnet spent his first years as a slave. Born in 1815 in Maryland, he escaped from slavery with his family at the age of nine. Garnet's best-known writing was a speech he gave in 1843, which he called "An Address to the Slaves of the United States of America." In this speech, Garnet advocated the use of violence to overturn the slave system. Using language and emotional appeals that would have pleased David Walker, Garnet laid down a challenge to the slaves of the South. "IT IS YOUR SOLEMN AND IMPERATIVE DUTY," he thundered, "TO USE EVERY MEANS, BOTH MORAL, INTELLECTUAL, AND PHYSICAL, THAT PROMISES SUCCESS."[18]

Harper and Delany

Black women writers served the cause of abolition, too. Frances W. Harper, born in Maryland in 1825, was one example. Among the best-known African American writers of the period, Harper published dozens of poems and a few prose pieces. Many date from the years after the Civil War, but some of her most famous works were written while slavery was still very much alive. Harper's best-known poem, called "The Slave Mother," was written in 1854. It describes the feelings of a slave woman about to be separated from her son. "Heard you that shriek?" the poem begins,

It rose

So wildly in the air,

It seemed as if a burdened heart

Was breaking in despair.[19]

Another notable antislavery writer of the period was a man named Martin Delany. Delany was born in Virginia in 1812 and, like Walker and Harper, was never a slave. A man of many talents, Delany served at various times as a newspaper editor, a doctor, a judge, and a politician. Unlike many other blacks of the time, Delany doubted that abolition would raise African Americans to a position of equality with whites. In accord with this belief, Delany published a book in 1852 in which he encouraged black people to leave the United States altogether.

Delany's wish was for African Americans to settle in places where there were few white people, if indeed any. Out of the range of whites, he argued, blacks could establish their own governments and traditions. "Every people should be the originators of their own destiny," he wrote, "the projectors of their own schemes, and the creators of the events that lead to their destiny."[20] Delany was not the only thinker of his time who saw mass emigration as the solution to the problem of race in America. Several white writers and politicians of the time offered similar proposals. Logistically, however, it was not possible to send all American blacks elsewhere, and Delany's wish never became reality.

Frances W. Harper was one of the best-known African American writers of the nineteenth century.

Slave Narratives

The majority of abolitionist writers of this period had spent most of their lives, if not all, in freedom. That was not the case, however, for the authors of another form of antislavery literature—the slave narrative. Slave narratives could be book-length volumes or mere pamphlets. In either case, they were sold to the public

Moses Roper

———————————◼———————————

Moses Roper was born into slavery around 1816. Mistreated by a succession of masters, Roper made several unsuccessful attempts to escape to the North. In 1834, however, he made his way to Savannah, Georgia, where he passed himself off as white and signed on as a deckhand on a ship. He eventually went to England and wrote a narrative of his years in slavery, which was published in 1838. This excerpt from his narrative describes one of his earliest attempts to run to freedom. The excerpt begins as Roper tries to evade some white men who are pursuing him.

I then came to a rail fence, which I found very difficult to get over, but breaking several rails away, I effected my object [that is, succeeded]. They then called upon me to stop, more than three times, and I not doing so, they fired after me, but the pistol only snapped [that is, it did not actually fire]. This is according to law: after three calls they may shoot a runaway slave. Soon after[,] the one on the horse came up with me, and catching hold of the bridle of my horse, pushed the pistol to my side; the other soon came up, and breaking off several stout branches from the trees, they gave me about a hundred blows. They did this very near to a planter's house; the gentleman was not at home, but his wife came out, and begged them not to *kill* me *so near the house*; they took no notice of this, but kept on beating me.

Quoted in Richard Barksdale and Keneth Kinnamon, eds. *Black Writers of America: A Comprehensive Anthology.* New York: Macmillan, 1972.

as genuine accounts of slave life, written or dictated by a former slave who had either purchased his or her freedom or had escaped to the free North. The best of these books were strong indictments of the slave system, but they were also uplifting stories that showcased the strength, courage, and resilience of men and women who had once been held in bondage. The slave narrative was an important expression of African American literature in the years before the Civil War.

Not every slave narrative was the unvarnished truth. As Northern opinion swung more and more strongly against slavery in the 1840s and 1850s, some publishers began issuing narratives that were far more fiction than fact. Though the title pages of these works carried the names of former slaves, the real authors were professional writers who paid little attention to the slaves' actual experiences. Publishers knew their audiences, and they were aware that a narrative full of danger and drama would sell, regardless of its authenticity, while a narrative that lacked these features would not. Given the intense competition among publishers of the time to find an audience for their books, it is not surprising that some sacrificed the truth in favor of profits.

Some narratives, however, were authentic. A few were the work of former slaves who had learned to read and write as children or after reaching the North. Others were put together by ghostwriters who more or less took dictation from the slaves. In both cases, the events described in the books reflected the realities of slavery and the feelings of the slaves. They are extremely useful in providing modern-day readers with a sense of what it might have been like to be enslaved.

Many of the slave narratives contain accounts of the hardships and trauma of escaping to the North.

Slave narratives typically follow a standard format. Since the narratives were intended for an antislavery audience, the books usually began by describing the brutality of the slaveholders. Most of the violence in the books consisted of whippings and beatings, but the narratives detailed more severe cruelty as well. In some cases, the narrators nearly died at the hands of their tormentors. "He pour[ed] some tar on my head," wrote a slave named Moses Roper about a particularly cruel white man, "then rubbed it all over my face . . . and set it on fire."[21] Roper barely survived.

The second section of most slave narratives, in turn, described the slave's attempt to escape. This part of the narrative emphasized the physical and psychological terrors of the journey north. Fugitives most often traveled by night, sneaking through forests and swamps to avoid towns and main roads. They ran low on food, they suffered in cold and rain, and they knew that one mistake or one stroke of bad luck could result in capture. "I was hungry and began to feel the desperation of distress," wrote James Pennington about his harrowing journey from bondage in Maryland to freedom in Pennsylvania. "As I travelled I felt my strength failing and my spirits wavered; my mind was in a deep and melancholy dream."[22] Accounts like this were standard in slave narratives.

Olaudah Equiano

The slave narrative genre got its start in 1789, when a British publisher printed the memoirs of a man named Olaudah Equiano (sometimes known as Gustavus Vassa). Equiano's life was considered well worth recording. According to his narrative, Equiano was born in West Africa about 1745. Kidnapped and sold into slavery at the age of ten or eleven, he served a variety of African masters before being sold to white traders who eventually brought him to Virginia. Once in North America, Equiano impressed his owners with his talents and intelligence. Despite being a slave, he became literate and was taught business practices and navigational techniques. When Equiano reached his early twenties, he purchased his freedom, settled in England, and began campaigning for the end of slavery. He died in 1797.

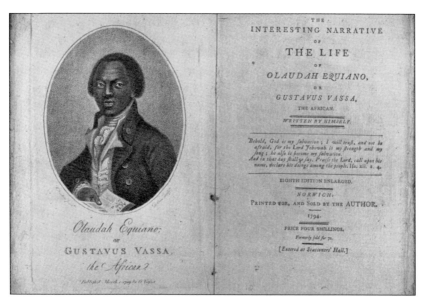

Olaudah Equiano's slave narrative was published in 1789. It started the slave narrative genre.

Equiano's memoir, entitled *The Life of Olaudah Equiano or Gustavus Vassa the African,* was a financial success. It went through eight printings in its first five years of publication, and it was widely read both in England and in the northern United States for many years thereafter. Its popularity was due to the book's quality. Equiano's life was compelling, and his story was well told, though overwritten by modern standards. It was by turns dramatic, tragic, hopeful, and shocking. Equiano described not only the realities of his life but gave a running account of his feelings as well. "All within my breast was tumult, wildness, and delirium!" Equiano wrote, for example, reliving the moment when he finally became free. "My feet scarcely touched the ground, for they were winged with joy."[23]

Equiano's book had two main purposes. One was religious. An ardent Christian who had been baptized into the faith while still enslaved, Equiano referred frequently in his memoir to his trust in God and to God's promise of heaven for believers. In this way, *The Life of Olaudah Equino* was an evangelical document: Equiano intended to spread the message of Jesus among his readers. The other purpose was political. As with later narratives, Equiano's work pointed up the evils of slavery. He hoped to enrage and horrify his audience, perhaps spurring them to join the fight for abolition. Accordingly, Equiano closed the book with a call to British officials to end England's involvement in the slave trade.

Later Narratives

Equiano's memoir set the stage for later slave narratives. Like Equiano's account, the narratives of the nineteenth century were religious as well as political. They included long descriptions of the evils of slavery, but they also assured readers of the mercy of the Christian God—both as a tool for evangelism and as a way to link the antislavery cause with Christian ideals. There were other similarities, too. Just as Equiano's book was

"Thou Boasted Land of Liberty"

James M. Whitfield was an African American who was born in New Hampshire in 1822. Whitfield worked as a barber much of his life, but his true interest was poetry. In 1853 he published a brief poem, "America," that neatly summed up the anger many Northern blacks of the time harbored toward the United States and its white citizens for their treatment of African Americans. "America, it is to thee," Whitfield's poem began,

> Thou boasted land of liberty,
> It is to thee I raise my song.
> Thou land of blood, and crime, and wrong.

Whitfield went on to describe the inhumanity of taking black people from Africa to labor as slaves, and to discuss the brutality with which most slaves were treated. African Americans, he concluded, had been unfairly

> Stripped of those rights which Nature's God
> Bequeathed to all the human race,
> Bound to a petty tyrant's nod,
> Because he wears a paler face.

Quoted in Donald A. Petesch. *A Spy in the Enemy's Country.* Iowa City: University of Iowa Press, 1989.

packed with drama and suspense, for example, so too were the works of later narrators. And virtually every narrative, regardless of when it was published, ended on a positive note, with the author gaining his or her freedom and leaving slavery behind forever.

There were two points, however, in which later narratives differed from Equiano's. For one, Equiano's memoir described his childhood in Africa and his terrifying journey across the Atlantic. These events were missing from most nineteenth-century slave narratives, because the authors of these works had typically been born in North America and had no direct connection to an African homeland. The other difference had to do with how the narrators became free. Equiano, of course, bought his freedom, but few later writers did the same. Most often they ran away from their homes and owners, leaving their former lives behind in a dangerous and often dramatic quest for freedom.

Indeed, the descriptions of escapes in the narratives of the 1800s are often astonishing. In 1860, for instance, former slaves William and Ellen Craft published a book called *Running a Thousand Miles for Freedom*. The text focused on the Crafts' audacious escape by train from the slave state of Georgia to the free state of Pennsylvania. Ellen, a light-skinned woman, disguised herself as a young white man, a Southern planter traveling to Philadelphia for a medical consultation. William, much darker than his wife, played the role of the young planter's slave. After several narrow escapes, including a moment when Ellen—who could neither read nor write—was asked to sign a document, the couple finally arrived in Pennsylvania. "Thank God, William, we are safe!"[24] Ellen cried out, according to the book, when it was clear that they were free.

A similarly dramatic tale involved a Virginia slave named Henry Brown. Resolving to escape after his wife and children were separated from him and sold to a slave trader, Brown had friends pack him inside a small crate and mail him to a Northern antislavery society. The trip, completed mainly by train, was excruciating. During the twenty-eight-hour journey Brown had little fresh air, hardly any room to move, and practically no food or water. The psychological horror may even have been worse than the physical discomfort. "A cold sweat now covered me from head to foot," he wrote at one point, describing his feelings of panic at the thought that his escape attempt might not succeed. "Death seemed my inevitable fate."[25] But Brown survived and reached his destination. He became known as "Box" Brown, and his account of the escape was published in both England and America.

Frederick Douglass

Probably the best-known of all slave narratives—and the most literary as well—was a book entitled *Narrative of the Life of Frederick Douglass, an American Slave*. Douglass, who wrote the book without the aid of a ghostwriter, was one of the most remarkable Americans in history. Born into slavery in Maryland about 1818, Douglass learned to read as a boy. As a young adult, Douglass decided to run north to freedom. Though his first two attempts were unsuccessful, he reached Philadelphia and freedom on his third try, in 1838. He went on to become a well-known abolitionist and political leader who was especially famous for his public-speaking abilities. In all likelihood he was the most famous African American of his time.

Douglass published his autobiography in 1845. In some ways, Douglass's narrative was like others in the genre. For example, Douglass described the brutal punishments he received at the hands of his masters, and he was unsparing in his account of the reality of slavery. Douglass also described his desire for freedom, though his narrative was not forthcoming about the details of his final, successful escape attempt. He feared that a thorough description would hurt other slaves who wanted to make escapes of their own. "I would keep the merciless slaveholder profoundly ignorant of the means of flight adopted by the slave,"[26] he wrote, explaining why he made this decision.

Although there were many similarities, Douglass's autobiography did differ from the standard slave narratives of the day. One was Douglass's writing skill. He wrote in clear, careful prose, resulting in a book of such quality that some critics doubted that Douglass was the actual author. Where ideas were concerned, moreover, Douglass's memoir moved beyond the simple discussions of slavery and faith prominent in most slave narratives. While Douglass was a devout Christian, for example, he viewed

Frederick Douglass's *Narrative of the Life of Frederick Douglass* was published in 1845. It is the best known of all slave narratives.

his religion more critically than most. In particular, he drew a sharp line between what he perceived as Christian ideals and the practices of the slaveholders. "I love the pure, peaceable, and impartial Christianity of Christ," he wrote in a postscript to his narrative. "I therefore hate the corrupt, slaveholding, women-whipping, cradle-plundering, partial and hypocritical Christianity of the land."[27]

Harriet Jacobs

In 1861, the year the Civil War began, a woman named Harriet Jacobs published a book called *Incidents in the Life of a Slave Girl*. Using the pseudonym Linda Brent, Jacobs described the often horrifying details of her life growing up in slavery. The book's importance lies partly in its frank discussion of Jacobs's own experiences, but it is also valuable for the insight it gives into the specific problems faced by slave women. In particular, the book tells of Jacobs's desperate attempts to ward off sexual advances from her owner and her sorrow and frustration at being unable to protect her children from harm. Both experiences, unfortunately, were common for slave women across the South.

This excerpt from Jacobs's book describes what happened when she initially rejected the advances of her master, Dr. Flint, whom she despised.

> My master met me at every turn, reminding me that I belonged to him, and swearing by heaven and earth that he would compel me to submit to him. If I went out for a breath of fresh air, after a day of wearied toil, his footsteps dogged me. If I knelt by my mother's grave, his dark shadow fell on me even there. The light heart which nature had given me became heavy with sad forebodings. . . . I longed for someone to confide in. I would have given the world to have laid my head on my grandmother's faithful bosom, and tell her all my troubles. But Dr. Flint swore he would kill me, if I was not as silent as the grave.

Harriet Jacobs. *Incidents in the Life of a Slave Girl*. Boston, 1861, p. 46.

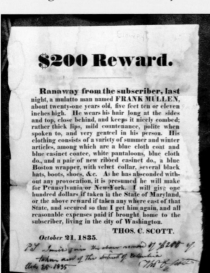

A runaway slave notice for Harriet Jacobs, like this one, was published in 1835. She would later recount her experiences in *Incidents in the Life of a Slave Girl,* published in 1861.

Douglass's subtly distinct attitudes were evident in other areas as well. His autobiography took up complex questions of racism, patriotism, and more, themes that also appeared in Douglass's later writings. Many of Douglass's words echoed those of black writers like Walker and Delany. But while these men were read primarily by African Americans, Douglass brought similar ideas to audiences that were largely white. "What, to the American slave, is your 4th of July?" he asked white listeners in a speech he gave in 1852. "To him, your celebration is a sham . . . your shouts of liberty and equality, hollow mockery."[28] Slave narratives rarely indicted all of American society in this way, preferring instead to blame Southern whites alone. As Douglass saw it, however, all of America was complicit in slavery. Whether this idea was popular with his audiences or not, he thought it was necessary to say and write what he believed.

Literature and History

From a literary perspective, the writings of Douglass, Walker, Equiano, and other African Americans of the early 1800s were certainly important. Douglass, in particular, was a remarkable writer whose eloquence was as evident in the 1840s as it is today. Walker and Garnet made excellent use of clear, plain language and rhetorical devices to stir up their readers. And Equiano, together with some other former slaves, not only invented a new genre, but wrote scenes of drama and suspense that rank among the most stirring of their time.

The best of these works not only added to the richness of the African American literary tradition but also brought black literature more fully into the mainstream of American writing as well. By exploring important moral, philosophical, and political questions, these writers captured the attention—and in many cases, the respect and admiration—of Northern whites. At the time of the American Revolution, white Americans frequently dismissed the notion that blacks could be authors. By the time of the Civil War, whites were more willing to accept that African Americans could produce literature—and great literature at that.

But important as the writings of these authors are to African American literature, their main significance lies in their impact on American history. Many factors led to the eventual outlawing of slavery following the Civil War, but among these factors was the rapid growth of the abolitionist movement in the North in the 1840s and 1850s. The increasingly strident arguments against slavery not only helped bring many Northerners to abolition, but caused Southern whites to respond in ways that hastened war between the two sections of the country—a war that eventually destroyed the slave system in America. The writings of Douglass, Harper, the Crafts, and other black authors were instrumental in spreading the abolitionist message and, by extension, were instrumental in bringing about the end of slavery. That is their greatest legacy.

Chapter Three

After the Civil War: 1865–1918

Following the end of the Civil War in 1865, the United States abolished slavery forever. After two centuries of legal oppression, African Americans had a stake in society at last. But abolition did not eliminate poverty, prejudice, and ignorance—especially in the South, where state and local governments kept blacks from voting, interfered with their schooling, and established a system of segregation, or the separation of the races. As the writings of African Americans before the Civil War had focused primarily on slavery, so did many black writers of the later 1800s and the early 1900s concentrate on the problems of black Americans of the time: the issues of poverty, illiteracy, racism, and more.

Charles Chesnutt

Prior to the Civil War, nonfiction was far and away the most common genre used by black authors. Writers such as Frederick Douglass, David Walker, and Olaudah Equiano made excellent use of autobiographical accounts and persuasive essays to express their ideas. In contrast, Phillis Wheatley and Frances Harper were among only a few blacks to publish fiction or poetry. Following the Civil War, however, the heavy focus

BLACK HERITAGE

Charles W. Chesnutt

41
USA

Charles Waddell Chesnutt was the best-known African American writer of fiction in the late nineteenth century. His works described the lives of ordinary black men and women and black culture and traditions.

on nonfiction began to change. Though autobiography and essays remained popular, a significant number of African American authors began producing poems, stories, and novels as well. In some ways, the period following the Civil War marks the beginning of black fiction and poetry.

The best-known African American writer of fiction in the late nineteenth century was an Ohio native named Charles W. Chesnutt. Born in 1858, Chesnutt published several novels and dozens of short stories. Chesnutt's fiction most often describes the lives of ordinary black men and women, and he was especially interested in themes of black culture and traditions. Several of his stories discuss the superstitions and religious practices of rural African Americans. Others are based in part on tales from black folklore.

Unlike many previous writers, Chesnutt's work was not overtly political. That did not mean, however, that he ignored issues of poverty or racism. On the contrary, Chesnutt used his fictional characters to make important political and social points. His 1899 book *The Conjure Woman*, for example, is largely made up of stories told by a former slave to a Northern white couple who have moved south following the Civil War. Many of the stories date from the days of slavery, and several clearly demonstrate the brutality of the slave era. The narrator rarely reveals his feelings about these stories, but Chesnutt does not hesitate to show the white couple's reactions. "What a system it was," the wife eventually exclaims, "under which such things were possible."[29] By having this criticism come from a white outsider rather than from a black participant, Chesnutt makes the indictment of slavery that much more powerful.

Chesnutt also used humor and satire to deliver deeper messages. One story tells of Dick Owens, the grown son of a wealthy slave owner in the years just before the Civil War. To impress his girlfriend, who believes him to be lazy and unmotivated, Dick resolves to do something daring: He will help Grandison, one of his father's many slaves, escape to Canada. He plans a tour of the North and talks his father into sending Grandison along as Dick's personal servant.

Grandison seems surprisingly content to be a slave. He spends his days bowing and grinning and assuring Dick that the free blacks of the North "ain'[t] half as well off as dey would be down South whar dey'd be 'preciated."[30] Still, Dick assumes that Grandison will run away the moment he has an opportunity—and Dick plans to give the young slave as many opportunities as necessary. Once in the North, however, Grandison time and again fails to run off. Professing fear of abolitionists and utter loyalty to

Up from Slavery

Booker T. Washington believed wholeheartedly that African Americans' greatest responsibility was to benefit their communities. As an educator, Washington urged his students to return to their hometowns rather than seeking their fortunes in the cities of the South. In this excerpt from his influential autobiography *Up from Slavery,* Washington explains his goal for his students at Tuskegee Institute, the school he helped found in Alabama.

We found that most of our students came from the country districts, where agriculture in some form or other was the main dependence of the people. We learned that about eighty-five percent of the coloured people in the Gulf states [states such as Alabama and Mississippi] depended upon agriculture for their living. Since this was true, we wanted to be careful not to educate our students out of sympathy with agricultural life, so that they would be attracted from the country to the cities, and yield to the temptation of trying to live by their wits. We wanted to give them such an education as would fit a large proportion of them to be teachers, and at the same time cause them to return to the plantation districts and show the people there how to put new energy and new ideas into farming, as well as into the intellectual and moral and religious life of the people.

Although some of Washington's ideas are out of fashion today, *Up from Slavery* remains a classic of American literature.

Booker T. Washington. *Up from Slavery.* New York: Doubleday, 1901.

Booker T. Washington was a writer and educator who believed that African Americans' greatest responsibility was to benefit their communities.

his masters, he refuses to leave. Dick is eventually forced to lead Grandison into Canadian territory and walk away when the slave is not looking. At last, he tells himself, Grandison is gone.

But he is wrong. A month or so after Dick returns home, Grandison appears on the doorstep. Why Grandison would voluntarily return to slavery is a mystery at first, but one night a few weeks later all becomes clear when Grandison disappears—and not just Grandison, but his wife, his parents, and his siblings as well. Grandison quickly leads his family members north and into Canada, following the route Dick unwittingly showed him. Grandison's apparent servility, as it turns out, was only a cover. By pretending to be what he was not, Grandison freed not just himself, but his entire family. The lesson of Chesnutt's story echoes a common lesson in black folklore: Despite a lack of power, blacks can still outwit their oppressors.

Paul Laurence Dunbar

Just as Charles Chesnutt was the leading African American novelist of the late 1800s, the leading African American poet of the time was a man named Paul Laurence Dunbar. Like Chesnutt, Dunbar was a native of Ohio. Born in 1872, Dunbar shared Chesnutt's interest in black culture and traditions, and much of his poetry celebrates this interest. An excellent example is a poem titled "When Malindy Sings," which describes the singing voice of Malindy, a fictional African American woman. "It seems holier dan [than] evenin'/When de solemn chu'ch bell rings," the poem's narrator writes, "[as] I sit an' ca'mly listen/While Malindy sings."[31] The poem honors the role of music in African American society and makes it clear that African Americans can produce great art.

Dunbar also wrote of the struggles faced by blacks as they tried to make their way in a world run largely by whites. One of his most famous works, "We Wear the Mask," discusses the need for blacks to cover their true feelings when dealing with the white majority. During this time period, whites typically expected African Americans to act happy and cheerful whether they were or not. Fearful of the consequences of showing other emotions, particularly anger, blacks usually obliged. To Dunbar, this was akin to putting on a mask that made it impossible to see the wearer clearly. As the first line of the poem puts it, "We wear the mask that grins and lies."[32]

Dunbar's concern, however, was not so much that the mask made it impossible for whites to see blacks for who they really were. His deeper worry was the effect that the mask had on the African Americans who metaphorically wore it. The psychological damage of not being able to express feelings, Dunbar argued, is appalling. As he wrote in the poem's conclusion:

We smile, but, O great Christ, our cries

To thee from tortured souls arise . . .

But let the world dream otherwise,

We wear the mask![33]

Poet and novelist Paul Laurence Dunbar. He wrote of the struggles faced by blacks as they tried to make their way in a white world.

The Blues

The blues was a musical form created by African Americans at the end of the 1800s and in the early 1900s. The typical blues song uses a series of rhyming couplets to describe feelings or a situation. Most blues songs focus on hardship and pain; common themes in blues lyrics include broken hearts, a lack of money, and the day-to-day difficulty of staying alive in a world that does not seem to care. Today, the lyrics to blues songs are often seen as a uniquely American art form.

Some blues songs have a single composer. W.C. Handy, a black bandleader from Alabama, was one of the earliest and most influential of these. He wrote the words and music to blues classics such as "Memphis Blues," "Yellow Dog Blues," and the well-known, often-recorded "St. Louis Blues." Handy's connection to the blues is so strong, in fact, that he titled his autobiography *Father of the Blues*.

Though some blues songs were written by individual artists such as Handy, many others were created through the folk process—that is, by passing the songs on from one performer to another, each person making a few changes as it goes along. The lyric below, from a blues song called "When a Woman Blue," was created in this way. It was sung by black laborers in Texas in the early 1900s.

When a woman blue, when a
  woman blue,
She hang her little head and cry—
When a woman blue, when a woman
  blue,
She hang her little head and cry . . .
When a man get blue
He grab a railroad train and ride.

Carl Sandburg. *The American Songbag*, New York: Harcourt Brace & Co., 1927, p. 236

W. C. Handy wrote "St. Louis Blues" and many other popular blues songs. He is often called the father of the blues.

James Weldon Johnson

Dunbar was not the only African American to earn widespread attention for his poetry. He was joined by one of his contemporaries, a writer named James Weldon Johnson. Born in Florida in 1871, Johnson was gifted in many areas besides poetry. At various times he was a schoolteacher, a college professor, and a book editor; he also wrote songs, worked for the U.S. Foreign Service, and served as president of a black political organization. During his lifetime, he was widely recognized as one of the most talented figures of black America, and today he is often considered one of the top minds of his generation.

Like both Chesnutt and Dunbar, Johnson had a deep interest in black folklore, culture, and history, and these themes are at the center of most of Johnson's work. He is especially well known today for a 1908 poem that celebrates black spirituals. To Johnson, the spirituals—both words and music—represented perhaps the greatest artistic achievement of the New World. "O black and unknown bards [poets] of long ago," the poem begins, "How came your lips to touch the sacred fire?" Johnson found the creation of the spirituals all the more remarkable given that these works had sprung from the victims of slavery. It was astonishing, he wrote, that an oppressed people could "find within its deadened heart to sing/These songs of sorrow, love, and faith, and hope."[34]

Johnson believed wholeheartedly that blacks needed to understand their unique history. Accordingly, he edited one of the first books of African American poetry and wrote several important essays about the African American past. He also wrote an influential poem, "Lift Ev'ry Voice and Sing," which focused on the black past and present. First published as a poem in 1900 and set to music by Johnson's brother Rosamond several years later, the poem urges blacks to understand and take pride in their heritage. In couplets such as "Stony the road we trod/Bitter the chast'ning rod," Johnson acknowledges the obstacles African Americans have faced over the years. Yet at the same time, the poem is optimistic. Johnson refers, for example, to the "gleam of our bright star" and "the hope that the present has brought us"[35]—and as a devout Christian, reminds his audience that God is with them.

In the years since it was written, "Lift Ev'ry Voice and Sing" has inspired and comforted generations of African Americans. It is frequently sung in churches as a hymn, and even today it remains a common feature of meetings and celebrations held in black communities. Indeed, the piece has become so popular and

James Weldon Johnson was not only a writer and poet but also a songwriter, book editor, schoolteacher, college professor, and political leader.

so beloved that it has often been called the "Negro national anthem."[36] Johnson's grasp of the sweep of African American history, together with his message to look to the future with hope and anticipation, gave his poem strength and meaning. Even now, more than a century after it was written, the piece is a classic of African American literature.

Washington and DuBois

Though fiction and poetry were becoming a vital part of African American literature after the Civil War, nonfiction remained an essential genre as well. Several prominent blacks wrote essays, autobiographical accounts, and histories during this period. Chief among these writers were two men whose backgrounds, temperaments, and outlooks were very different, but who shared a desire

Booker T. Washington founded the prestigious Tuskegee Institute in Tuskegee, Alabama, in 1891.

to improve the lives of African Americans everywhere. One of these men was Booker T. Washington; the other, W.E.B. DuBois. The most influential black writers of their time, Washington and DuBois served in many ways as the political, cultural, and moral leaders of black America in the period between the Civil War and World War I.

The older of these two men, Washington was born into slavery on a Virginia plantation in 1856. From early on he recognized that blacks were not treated as full members of society, and as an adult he resolved to try to change that. Washington hoped that white leaders would someday be ready to accept blacks as their political and social equals. At the same time, Washington was a pragmatist, and he suspected that such acceptance was a long way off. Rather than push for voting rights, an immediate end to segregation, and other political changes, Washington decided to use another strategy: education.

In 1891 Washington moved to Alabama and became the founding president of Tuskegee Institute. This school was designed to prepare blacks for jobs in business, agriculture, and manufacturing. As Washington saw it, job training was essential to any effort to improve the lives of African Americans. Better job skills, he noted, would increase the earning power of blacks and would help African Americans move out of poverty. It would also show whites that African Americans could be more than farmhands and unskilled laborers. Once African Americans became economically self-sufficient, Washington argued, campaigns to establish voting and other rights for blacks might be successful. In the meantime, however, working toward these goals would have to wait.

A New Leader

In 1895 Washington presented his ideas in a speech to an integrated audience at an Atlanta business convention. "In all things that are purely social, [blacks and whites] can be as separate as the fingers," Washington said, "yet one as the hand in all things essential to mutual progress."[37] The speech catapulted Washington into the national spotlight and thrust him into the role of a leader of African Americans. Whites approved of his willingness not to press for immediate political and social rights; many blacks applauded Washington's determination to increase their standard of living. Almost overnight Washington went from little known to famous.

Over the next few years Washington worked tirelessly for economic self-sufficiency. He lectured, wrote, and traveled widely to bring his message to blacks and whites across the country. In 1901 he published the most significant of his works, an autobiography called *Up from Slavery*. The book reflected Washington's general policy of emphasizing what blacks could do for themselves rather than bemoaning the evils of society. Even at the beginning of the narrative, Washington took pains to point out that while he and his fellow slaves had reacted joyfully to the news that they were finally free, "there was no feeling of bitterness" toward the whites who had enslaved them. On the contrary, he added, "there was pity among the slaves for our former owners."[38]

Up from Slavery went on to describe Washington's education, his leadership at Tuskegee Institute, and the speech that had brought him national attention. It also made clear Washington's basic philosophy. "I believe it is the duty of the Negro," he wrote, "to deport himself modestly in regard to political claims. . . . I think that the according of the full exercise of political rights is going to be a matter of natural, slow growth."[39] Popular among whites as well as many blacks, Washington's autobiography was well written and influential. It set a tone for public debate on racial issues not only for the time but for many years to come. For this, and also for its portrayal of Washington's remarkable success in the face of prejudice and adversity, it continues to rank as one of the great works of African American literature.

W.E.B. DuBois

If Washington represented one type of black leader, DuBois—born in Massachusetts in 1868—represented the opposite extreme. As a scholar, political activist, and editor, DuBois disagreed vehemently with Washington's willingness to wait for social and political equality. DuBois argued that Washington's methods would never lead to full citizenship for blacks. To him, political change was the first and most important goal. "By every civilized and peaceful method," DuBois wrote in a direct rebuke to Wash-

Scholar, editor, writer, and political activist W.E.B DuBois disagreed with Washington's philosophy of waiting for social and political equality. He believed the struggle for equality must be first and foremost.

ington and his policies, "we must strive for the rights which the world accords to men."[40]

In 1903 DuBois published a book of essays called *The Souls of Black Folk*. Many of the essays described his approach to the problem of racism. In contrast to Washington, DuBois demanded basic rights for African Americans, and he demanded them without delay. In his eyes, black leaders were obligated to push for these rights. Much of *The Souls of Black Folk* was dedicated to DuBois's opinions on this subject and his disagreements—sometimes sharp, sometimes more muted—with Washington and other blacks who adopted his perspective.

Like *Up from Slavery,* though, *The Souls of Black Folk* was much more than a political document. Many African Americans found that the book neatly captured their experience of being black in a largely white world. DuBois, they found, described their sorrows and their dreams; he understood and accepted both the challenges and the joys of being African American. Blacks, DuBois wrote at one point, had a "sense of always looking at one's self through the eyes of others, of measuring one's soul by the tape of a world that looks on in amused contempt and pity."[41]

"Lift Ev'ry Voice and Sing"

In this excerpt from Maya Angelou's memoir *I Know Why the Caged Bird Sings,* Angelou recalls the pride she and her classmates felt while singing James Weldon Johnson's "Lift Ev'ry Voice and Sing" at her eighth grade graduation from a segregated school in rural Arkansas.

Every child I knew had learned that song with his ABC's and along with "Jesus Loves Me This I Know." But I personally had never heard it before. Never heard the words, despite the thousands of times I had sung them. Never thought they had anything to do with me. . . . And now I heard, really for the first time:

"We have come over a way that with tears has been watered,

We have come, treading our path through the blood of the slaughtered. . . ."

We were on top again. As always, again. We survived. The depths had been icy and dark, but now a proud sun spoke to our souls. I was no longer simply a member of the proud graduating class of 1940; I was a proud member of the wonderful, beautiful Negro race.

Maya Angelou. *I Know Why the Caged Bird Sings.* New York: Random House, 1969.

On the Horizon

Washington died in 1915, but DuBois continued his advocacy for African Americans for decades to come. He lived until 1963, leaving behind dozens of writings about politics, history, and what it means to be black. Today, most black critics hold DuBois's work in higher esteem than they do Washington's, believing that the passage of time has demonstrated that DuBois's ideas were more effective than Washington's. DuBois stands out as one of the giants of African American literature—and of American history as well.

But DuBois is not alone in this distinction. Washington's memoir, though politically out of fashion today, remains an inspiring tale of a man who rose from slavery to become a leader of his people. From the folkloric images of Chesnutt's *The Conjure Woman* to the racial pride of Johnson's poetry, from the political wisdom of DuBois to the keen insight of Dunbar, African American literature had come a long way since the early works of Phillis Wheatley and Jupiter Hammon. It had broadened its focus, branched into new literary forms, and come to appeal more and more to white readers. Perhaps most of all, black literature of this period had become ever more supportive and reflective of the black experience. The works of writers such as Washington and Johnson had brought African American literature to a new level. The next generations of African American writers would take these themes and develop them further still.

Chapter Four

The Harlem Renaissance: 1918–1940

The 1920s, often nicknamed the Roaring Twenties, represented the most prosperous decade in American history to that point. Business boomed, jobs were easy to find, and the standard of living increased, it seemed, every year. The twenties were also a time of enormous—and sudden—cultural change. Women cut their hair short; jazz music became popular. The country adopted new heroes, such as baseball star Babe Ruth and movie actor Rudolph Valentino. The carefree, upbeat atmosphere of the period led one observer to call the twenties the "Era of Wonderful Nonsense."[42]

The events of the 1920s formed the backdrop to one of America's greatest literary movements. Known as the Harlem Renaissance, the movement got its start—and its name—in Harlem, a heavily black community in New York City that was a magnet for African American writers and artists of the time. Never before in American history had so many black writers come together to share ideas, support one another, and work toward common goals. Through the 1920s and into the 1930s, the writers of the Harlem Renaissance produced a remarkable array of poems, plays, stories, novels, essays, and more. In many ways, the Harlem Renaissance marks the beginning of modern African American literature.

Harlem

Located on the northern part of Manhattan Island, Harlem became a destination for African Americans during the early 1900s. Blacks who already lived in New York City were attracted to the neighborhood's wide streets, solid houses, and relatively low rents. Migrants from the rural South, searching for better lives and higher-paying jobs, soon settled in the community as well. By 1920 about one-third of the population of central Harlem was African American, and in the next ten years that proportion would more than double.

Many of Harlem's new African American residents were poor and uneducated. They eked out a meager living working for low wages as laborers or servants. But Harlem also attracted well-educated, better-off blacks. These men and women viewed the neighborhood as something unique, a place within the country's biggest metropolis where African Americans of every background could join together and build a new and exciting community. As James Weldon Johnson wrote in 1925, "Harlem is not merely a Negro colony or community, it is a city within a city, the greatest Negro city in the world."[43] By the early 1920s the community had become established as a center of African American culture. In Harlem, novelist and critic Arna Bontemps wrote, it was "fun to be a Negro."[44] The literature that came out of Harlem reflected this sense of excitement and fun in many ways.

Charles S. Johnson

The person perhaps most responsible for the Harlem Renaissance was an African American scholar named Charles S. Johnson. Born in 1893, Johnson was a sociologist by training, and he was a strong advocate against racism at a time when few blacks felt safe speaking out. In the early 1920s, Johnson came to Harlem to work for a black advocacy group called the National Urban League. One of his duties was to edit the organization's new magazine, *Opportunity: A Journal of Negro Life*. At first, Johnson filled the magazine

Harlem's Lenox Avenue in the 1920s. Harlem would become the center of one of America's greatest literary and musical movements.

with scholarly articles. But soon he decided to emphasize the arts in his journal. Accordingly, *Opportunity* began to publish short stories and poems written by black authors, along with theater reviews and other articles about the arts.

Johnson was impressed with the talents of the people he recruited to write for his magazine, and he decided to bring their work to the attention of white publishers. Though few mainstream presses had printed fiction or poetry by blacks in the past, Johnson believed that the new generation of publishers might be ready to change this policy. Moreover, Johnson's academic background and work with the National Urban League gave him connections to influential members of white society. Johnson was well placed to bring African American writing into the broader literary culture.

In March 1924 Johnson gave a party to celebrate the publication of a novel by a Harlem writer and editor named Jessie Fauset. The guests included many of the most promising young writers in Harlem, along with veteran authors such as W.E.B. DuBois. But not all the guests were African American. Johnson had invited white authors and publishers as well, and several of these men were in attendance. Johnson hoped that the white guests would be impressed by the black writers they met and perhaps consider publishing some of their works.

Charles S. Johnson, a sociologist by trade, is credited as the one most responsible for the Harlem Renaissance.

In this goal Johnson was wildly successful. At the party, a white editor named Carl Van Doren gave a speech in which he strongly urged white publishers to seek out black authors. "What American literature decidedly needs at this moment is color, music, [and] gusto," he argued. "If the Negroes are not in a position to contribute these items, I do not know what Americans are."[45] In accord with Van Doren's suggestion, many publishers and editors at the party showed great interest in learning more about Harlem's writers and their work. The editor of *Harper's Magazine*

Jean Toomer

Jean Toomer, a mixed-race poet and novelist, was born in the District of Columbia in 1894. Toomer was a major figure in the Harlem Renaissance. He was best known for a novel published in 1923 that he called *Cane*. *Cane* included descriptions of black life in the rural South as well as in the urban North. Lyrically written and moving back and forth between prose, poetry, and drama, *Cane* was an immediate success; critics praised the novel for its realistic depiction of African American culture and its beautiful language. Though not read as often today as when it was first published, it remains a classic of black literature.

Oddly, though, *Cane*'s author was never comfortable with his racial heritage. He resisted being classified as a black writer. In his essays, especially those published after *Cane*, Toomer argued that he was both black *and* white, not simply African American, as most blacks and whites alike perceived him. On one occasion, in fact, he described his ancestry as a blend of various European ethnic groups—and then added, almost as an afterthought, that he carried some African heritage as well. It is unclear why he tried so hard to reject his African American ties. "To be a human being," theorizes a modern-day critic, "Toomer felt that he had to efface [eliminate] his mask of blackness, the cultural or racial trace of difference, and embrace the utter invisibility of being an American." Despite his attempt to carve a racial identity of his own, however, Toomer is still recognized as an important figure in the Harlem Renaissance as well as one of the finest writers of his time.

Quoted in William S. McConnell. *Harlem Renaissance*. San Diego: Greenhaven, 2003.

went even further: After hearing a young writer named Countee Cullen read some of his poetry at the celebration, he immediately agreed to publish Cullen's work in an upcoming issue.

The Harlem Renaissance did not begin on the night of Johnson's party. To a large degree, the movement had already begun. Most of the authors who made their names during the movement were already writing, and some, like Fauset, had achieved recognition for their work. Still, that evening in 1924 brought the movement into the public eye, attracted new writers to Harlem, and helped establish a connection among the literary figures of the black community. Over the next few years, encouraged by Johnson and a black editor named Alain Locke, Harlem-based writers sold their novels to white publishers and placed their poetry and essays in national magazines. A barrier had been broken. The Harlem Renaissance was under way.

A Diverse Movement

The Harlem Renaissance is a difficult movement to characterize. In one sense, the movement was quite cohesive. The writers who made up the movement largely viewed themselves as being part of a group. Many of them lived within a radius of just a few miles. They moved in the same social and professional circles; they supported each other's work; they pushed as a unit for greater recognition in the black community and beyond.

At the same time, however, the works produced by these writers often had very little in common with one another. The men and women of the Harlem Renaissance wrote in a hodgepodge of genres and made use of an enormous variety of literary forms and styles. Cullen was best known for his poetry, Fauset for her novels. Zora Neale Hurston, born in Alabama in 1891, was trained as a folklorist; her works include collections of traditional African American tales. Langston Hughes, an exceptionally versatile writer, published poetry, novels, short stories, plays, and nonfiction. While some literary movements in American history have focused on a specific genre, such as drama, poems, or essays, the Harlem Renaissance included all of these and more.

These disparities made sense. The writers of the Harlem Renaissance were not all alike by any means. Though they were all black, they had wildly different experiences, interests, and

Poet Countee Cullen grew up in an upper-middle-class home in Harlem.

backgrounds, and sometimes the differences in upbringing were great indeed. Wealth, education, and social status, for example, were important dividers. Poet Cullen, for example, grew up in an upper-middle-class Harlem household as the son of a respected minister. Hughes, in contrast, grew up poor; his father abandoned his family, and Hughes was raised in part by his grandmother while his mother traveled to find work. Cullen earned a graduate degree while many other writers of the movement lacked a college degree—and in some cases, had never been to college at all.

Geographic origin divided the writers of the Harlem Renaissance, too. Some, such as Cullen, came from the East, while Hughes was a Midwesterner, and Hurston grew up in the South. Many came from New York, Los Angeles, or other urban areas, but others grew up in small towns or even in rural areas. Geography affected racial diversity as well. Hurston was raised in a community populated entirely by blacks, whereas Hughes was one of just two black students in his eighth grade graduating class.

For that matter, some of the writers of the Harlem Renaissance had roots outside the United States. Poet and novelist Claude McKay, for example, was born and raised in Jamaica and did not come to the United States until his early twenties. And novelist Nella Larsen, the child of a white European mother and a black father from the Caribbean, grew up partly in the United States and partly in Denmark. Given the differences in geography, education, background, and experience, it is easy to understand why the Harlem Renaissance represented such a variety of styles and genres.

Styles, Forms, and Voice

The diversity of styles is not hard to see. The poetry of Cullen, for example, uses traditional structures and language. Many of his poems are sonnets, a strict fourteen-line form used by John Keats, William Shakespeare, and other earlier English poets. Cullen's sonnets are easily distinguishable from those of Keats or Shakespeare because of their topics and themes. "Yet do I marvel at this curious thing," he wrote in a sonnet exploring what it meant to be African American, "To make a poet black, and bid him sing!"[46] In style and structure, though, several generations of English-language poets would have appreciated Cullen's verses. Indeed, modern critic Lorenzo Thomas describes Cullen's sonnets as "fluent and flawless."[47]

Compared with Cullen and several other writers of the Harlem Renaissance, Hughes was much more experimental in his approach to poetry. Hughes was best known for his free verse—poetry in which rhyme and meter are not important. Even in his earliest work Hughes was already playing with new structures and ideas. His first published poem, printed when Hughes was just nineteen, ended with the lines

I've known rivers,

Ancient, dusky rivers.

My soul has grown deep like the rivers.[48]

Some poets of the period made extensive use of artistic forms from black culture. The blues, for example, was a relatively new musical style in the early 1920s. Associated largely with black musicians in Mississippi and nearby parts of the South, it had spread into northern cities by the time the Harlem Renaissance began. Blues lyrics typically focused on the difficulties of life, and blues songs followed a rigid format in which the first and second lines were the same and the third line rhymed with the first two. Several of the best-known poems of the Harlem Renaissance, including Hughes's "The Weary Blues," were written in this new African American style.

Just as the forms and styles varied from one poet to the next, the structures and subjects used by novelists of the Harlem Renaissance differed, too. Some writers, such as Fauset, wrote largely about well-off and influential blacks in cities like Philadelphia and New York. Others, like Hurston, were more inclined to write about the lives of African Americans in the rural South. Still others, notably McKay, focused their attention on lower-class blacks in urban areas.

Each of these writers, however, used dialogue that matched their characters' lives. The well-educated people of Fauset's work, for instance, use standard English, while the characters in Hurston's and McKay's books use expressions and grammatical constructions typical of lower-class blacks of the time. "Ah ain't been near de place, man," says one character in Hurston's novel *Their Eyes Were Watching God*. "Ah been down tuh de lake tryin' tuh ketch me uh fish."[49]

The Theme of Race

Despite all the diversity of the Harlem Renaissance, one powerful similarity linked the work of every one of the men and women who were part of the movement. That element was race. The writers of

Langston Hughes Makes His Mark

Langston Hughes was first published in 1921, shortly before his twentieth birthday, when his poem "The Negro Speaks of Rivers" appeared in the magazine *Crisis*. Though the poem is recognized as a classic today, it did not bring Hughes instant fame—or indeed much fame at all. Over the next few years, in fact, Hughes had difficulty getting anything else published. Between 1921 and 1925 he worked at a variety of unskilled jobs, writing when time permitted and hoping to be able to make a living as a writer someday.

In 1925 Hughes was working in the dining room of a Washington hotel. One of the hotel's guests that year was a noted American poet named Vachel Lindsay. Eager for feedback on his work, and hopeful of making contacts within the writing world, Hughes approached Lindsay one evening as he ate. He handed Lindsay a sampling of his own poetry and asked for the poet's reaction. Though annoyed by the interruption, Lindsay agreed to read Hughes's work—and was deeply impressed.

Lindsay's support helped boost Hughes's confidence. Later that year, Hughes entered a poetry contest sponsored by another African American publication, *Opportunity*. Hughes's poem "The Weary Blues" won first prize, finally bringing him the attention he sought. "One night Langston Hughes was just one of the bus boys of the Wardman Park Hotel," an Iowa newspaper reported shortly after the prize was announced. "Next day he was a well-known poet."

"Won Prize for Poem." *Rock Valley (IA) Bee*. December 25, 1925, p. 14.

Poet and writer Langston Hughes was best known for his free verse poetry.

the Harlem Renaissance were all of African descent, and in a racist nation this fact was of profound importance. Fauset and McKay, Hughes and Larsen—all were viewed as blacks first and writers second. Accordingly, the works of virtually every member of the movement discuss the experience of being black in America.

No two writers approached the theme of race in exactly the same way. Some wrote from a deeply political perspective. Their works lashed out at America and the laws and traditions that constricted blacks' opportunities. "[S]he feeds me bread of bitterness,"[50] McKay wrote angrily in a poem about the United States. McKay was more radical than most, but other writers of the movement echoed his sentiments. "I am the darker brother," wrote Hughes in his poem "I, Too." "They send me to eat in the kitchen/When company comes."[51]

Other works emphasized the struggles of African Americans. Sometimes these struggles stemmed from the racism of powerful whites who saw no need to treat blacks humanely. "Cora, bake three cakes for Mary's birthday tomorrow night," demands a white employer in a Hughes short story about an African American maid. "You Cora, give Rover a bath in that tar soap I bought."[52] Sometimes, though, the struggles had little direct relationship to white racism. Several novels of the period, for example, describe the damage caused to African American communities by prostitution, alcoholism, and drug use.

Still other writings of the Harlem Renaissance celebrate blacks and black culture. These stories and poems portray African America in a positive light and encourage black readers to take pride in their racial identity. In "I, Too," after likening the African American experience to the feelings of children refused seats at the dinner table, Hughes foresees a different attitude in years ahead. "They'll see how beautiful I am," the narrator predicts confidently, referring to white people, "and be ashamed."[53] Another example is Larsen's novel *Passing*. The mixed-race central character in the novel pretends at first to have no African ancestry at all, but ultimately embraces her black heritage as well. "You don't know, you can't realize how I want to see Negroes," she tells a friend, "to be with them again, to talk with them, to hear them laugh."[54]

No writer of the period played up the theme of black pride more than Hurston. Hurston's fiction is full of black characters who, though flawed, have great strengths. African Americans can be strong, smart, and brave, Hurston tells her black readers again and again, and being African American is something to take pride in—not something to be hidden or ashamed of. Her story "Drenched in Light," for instance, tells of a young black girl

Novelist Zora Neale Hurston's works were about the lives of African Americans in the rural South.

Like many black writers at the time, Jessie Fauset was viewed as a black first and a writer second.

named Isis, whose delight in the world makes a deep impression on a well-off white woman. "I want brightness and this Isis is joy itself," the woman exclaims. "I want a little of her sunshine to soak into my soul."[55]

In keeping with their emphasis on race, many writers of the Harlem Renaissance looked to Africa for inspiration and identity. "What is Africa to me?" Cullen asked in his poem "Heritage," exploring the meaning of Africa to a man "three centuries removed/From the land his father loved."[56] Despite their attraction to Africa, however, most writers of the movement ultimately saw themselves as Americans. Hughes, who visited Africa in the early 1920s, recognized that Africa was not the place that had shaped him. "I was . . . an American Negro who had loved the surface of Africa and the rhythms of Africa," Hughes wrote, "but I was not Africa, I was Chicago and Kansas City and Broadway and Harlem."[57]

"Free Within Ourselves"

As Johnson had hoped, the writers of the Harlem Renaissance were read not just by other African Americans, but by whites as well. By the end of the 1920s African American writing had become part of mainstream literature. Even newspapers in virtually all-white communities were taking notice of black writers and their talents. In 1929, for instance, a small-town Iowa paper reviewed Hughes's most recent volume of poetry. "Warmth and beauty and dreams enter into [these poems],"[58] the reviewer concluded, recommending the book to all readers.

The writers of the Harlem Renaissance were pleased that so many whites were drawn to their work. They benefited financially from a wider readership, and they recognized that the number of white readers indicated that society's attitudes toward blacks might be changing. Still, writing to please white people was not the goal. As Hughes wrote in an essay published in 1926, "We younger Negro artists who create now intend to express our individual dark-skinned selves without fear or shame. If white people are pleased we are glad. If they are not, it doesn't matter."[59] The greater purpose of the Harlem Renaissance, Hughes argued, was for writers to describe the hardships, joys, and dreams of American blacks, and to do so in a way that was honest and true.

Music and the Harlem Renaissance

The Harlem Renaissance was in large part a movement of writers, but it encompassed other art forms as well. That was particularly true of music. Star musicians from blues singer Ethel Waters to jazz trumpeter and singer Louis Armstrong presented concerts in venues such as the Apollo Theater on 125th Street. Ragtime pianist Eubie Blake, bandleader Duke Ellington, and vocalist Paul Robeson also were an important part of the Harlem musical world during the 1920s and 1930s.

No musical figure was more closely associated with Harlem than blues singer Bessie Smith. Smith grew up as part of a very poor family in the rural South, but the quality of her voice and the emotions she was able to express with it helped her become a famous entertainer. She was best known for performing classic blues songs such as "Nobody Knows You When You're Down and Out" and "St. Louis Blues." As historian Cary D. Wintz writes,

> Bessie Smith pretty much expressed the feelings of a generation of black listeners. She might sing of unfaithful men, of financial struggles, of flooding rivers destroying homes, of the unfairness of life, of having a loved one incarcerated; she sang with understanding, forbearance, and strength. And also at times with great, spirit-lifting zest—jubilation was to be found despite adversity and oppression.

Cary D. Wintz. *Harlem Speaks*. Naperville, IL: Sourcebooks, 2007, p. 176.

The diversity of the people who wrote during the Harlem Renaissance was perhaps the movement's most striking characteristic. At times, certainly, it was the movement's greatest weakness. The diversity of opinions and backgrounds often led to vocal disagreements. Author and critic Richard Wright disliked and criticized Hurston's novel *Their Eyes Were Watching God,* for example. The book, he wrote in a much-quoted review, "carries no theme, no message, no thought."[60] Older authors counseled younger writers to avoid controversial topics such as prostitution and alcoholism, and were angry when the younger writers ignored their advice. "*Home to Harlem* . . . nauseates me," wrote DuBois about one of McKay's books, "and after the dirtier parts of its filth I feel distinctly like taking a bath."[61]

Then again, the movement's diversity was also its greatest strength. The Harlem Renaissance was defined not by art or by style, but by time, geography, and most of all race. The tie that bound these men and women together was not their writing, but themselves. Despite the bickering, the writers of the Harlem Renaissance generally saw themselves as part of a movement—and acted as such. They read each other's work, learned from one another, and built on one another's achievements. They painted an increasingly full picture of what it was like to be black in America. And they wrote to help create a brighter future for African Americans. "We will build our temples for tomorrow, strong as we know how," Hughes wrote in a 1926 essay, "and we will stand on top of the mountain, free within ourselves."[62]

The Harlem Renaissance represented an impressive flowering of African American literature. But the movement did not last long. The Great Depression, which began in 1929, forced dozens of publishers out of business, limiting the market for black writers. As economic conditions worsened, Harlem became increasingly poor and shabby, its crime rates rising and its status as the center of African American life no longer secure. At the same time, too, the writers of the Harlem Renaissance began drifting apart, both personally and artistically. Some quarreled with each other, leaving rifts that never healed. A few stopped writing altogether. The rest no longer saw themselves as part of a movement. Historians differ about when the Harlem Renaissance came to an end, but most agree that by 1939, the movement was over. The next great period of African American literature, however, was not long in coming.

Chapter Five

Through the Civil Rights Struggle: 1940–1969

In the 1940s, a new African American literary movement led by a new generation of black authors began to take shape. More overtly political than the Harlem Renaissance and more focused on black history and racial pride than the literature of the nineteenth century, the new movement had roots in the literature of earlier times. But the writers of this period had an even more important influence: the growing African American struggle for equality, known as the civil rights movement. By the beginning of the 1950s this new movement had established itself as a potent force, and it would remain so until the close of the 1960s. In this era, art and politics combined to produce a new literature: by turns angry, sad, and celebratory, and always uniquely African American.

Raceless Literature

Like the writers of the Harlem Renaissance, the African American authors of the 1940s and early 1950s were a diverse group. Many of them, however, did share a goal: the goal of assimilation. Their intent was to move into the mainstream and become known as American writers and not simply as African American writers. Some critics have called this universal writing or raceless writing. These men and women tried to avoid writing styles, language, or subject matter that could be seen as obviously African American. The aim of the black writer, a black critic wrote in 1949, should be to become "an American writer as free as any [other American] to tap the rich literary resources of our land and its people."[63]

Writer Ann Petry was one of the black writers who worked with nonracial themes in her novels.

To be sure, some of this sentiment was present during the 1920s as well. Langston Hughes, after all, emphasized his identity as an American; Countee Cullen and Claude McKay claimed traditional English poetry as part of their own heritage. But in the years immediately following World War II, many black writers downplayed race and racial issues in their writing. Among the most prominent of these was Georgia native Frank Yerby, a writer of historical novels about topics like medieval Europe and classical Greece. For Yerby, this broad thematic focus was a recipe for success. In 1946 his novel *The Foxes of Harrow* reached the best-seller lists, the first book by an African American author to do so.

Other writers of the period also worked with nonracial themes. Ann Petry, who was born in 1911, grew up in a small Connecticut town populated largely by whites. Though her first novel dealt with a poor black woman in Harlem, her second novel, published in 1947, was set in a New England town similar to the one where she grew up. It contained few African American characters and was not specifically concerned with those characters' struggles and dreams. And in 1948 Zora Neale Hurston, remembered today for the strength of her black characters and her abiding interest in African American folklore, published a novel, *Seraph on the Suwanee*, that featured white characters.

Richard Wright

Even as many black writers were moving further into the mainstream during the 1940s, a few continued to focus on African Americans and their struggles against a white world. One of these authors was Richard Wright. Born in Mississippi in 1908, Wright was publishing stories and essays by the early 1930s. In 1940 Wright published a novel, *Native Son*, which is widely considered a classic. Indeed, it appears on several modern-day lists of great English-language novels compiled by literary critics. For example, *Native Son* is included on *Time* magazine's list of the best novels since 1923, and in 1998 the Modern Library ranked it as one of the twenty best novels of the twentieth century.

Growing up in Mississippi, Wright experienced plenty of racism, and he worked themes of racial prejudice into his writings. *Native Son,* for example, tells the story of Bigger Thomas, a young man from a poor urban neighborhood. Bigger is frequently in

"They Won't Stand for It"

No book of the 1940s painted a more realistic picture of American race relations than Richard Wright's autobiography, *Black Boy*. Wright's themes included an examination of how the expectations of white Americans often affected the behavior of American blacks. In this excerpt, Wright gets a lesson from Griggs, a black friend, in how he should act around white people.

> "White people want you out of their way." [Griggs] pronounced the words slowly so that they would sink into my mind. . . . "You act around white people as if you didn't know that they were white. And they *see* it."
>
> "Oh, Christ, I can't be a slave," I said hopelessly.
>
> "But you've got to eat," he said.
>
> "Yes, I got to eat."
>
> "Then start acting like it," he hammered at me, pounding his fist in his palm. "When you're in front of white people, *think* before you act, *think* before you speak. Your way of doing things is all right among *our* people, but not for *white* people. They won't stand for it."
>
> I stared bleakly into the morning sun. I was nearing my seventeenth birthday and I was wondering if I would ever be free of this plague [of racism]. What Griggs was saying was true, but it was simply utterly impossible for me to calculate, to scheme, to act, to plot all the time. I would remember to dissemble [pretend] for short periods, then I would forget and act straight and human again, not with the desire to harm anyone, but merely forgetting the artificial status of race and class.

Richard Wright. *Black Boy*. New York: Harper, 1945, p. 218.

Richard Wright's 1940 novel *Native Son* is considered a classic of American literature.

trouble with the law, which Wright attributes partly to Bigger's bad choices, but also to the pervasive discrimination of the time. In the book, Bigger responds to his lack of opportunities with anger, violence, and despair. To Wright, Bigger stood for African Americans everywhere. "No American Negro exists," he wrote once, "who does not have his private Bigger Thomas living in his skull."[64]

Some critics and readers, including many whites, praised Wright's work for its realistic portrayal of African American life and its unflinching examination of racism. "Only a Negro could have written it," a reviewer for *Time* magazine stated about *Native Son*, "but until now no Negro has possessed either the talent or the daring to write it."[65] But others, including some notable black writers, were highly critical of Wright's work. Their particular concern was Wright's heavy focus on race. In an essay directed in large part at Wright and *Native Son*, for example, writer James Baldwin complained that by looking at Bigger solely as a black person, Wright made his main character a caricature, not a fully developed human being.

The criticism of Baldwin and other writers did not change Wright's way of thinking. In 1945 Wright published an influential autobiography, *Black Boy*. Like *Native Son*, *Black Boy* describes events clearly and realistically, making no attempt to hide the violence, poverty, and racism that Wright experienced throughout his life. In one sketch, for example, Wright describes working in a southern hotel where patrons and white staff members routinely bullied, threatened, and hit black employees. The laws and customs of the time and place forced the workers to put up with these behaviors—and to pretend that working at the hotel was a delight. "The maids, the hall-boys, and the bell-boys were all smiles," Wright explains. "They had to be."[66]

Into the Fifties

The black writers of the early 1950s drew from the themes of authors such as Wright, but they also were influenced by the assimilationist, raceless ideas of other African American writers. One of the best-known writers of this period was Baldwin, who had criticized the deeply racial tone of *Native Son*. Though Baldwin

James Baldwin shown here with his novel *No Name In the Street*.
Baldwin's 1952 novel *Go Tell It on the Mountain* is a semiautobiographical account of a black boy growing up in Harlem.

disapproved of Wright's stridency, Baldwin's fiction was known
for descriptions of urban blacks and African American life. His
novel *Go Tell It on the Mountain*, published in 1952, is an excellent
example. A semiautobiographical account of a black boy growing
up in Harlem, the book drew readers into the details of African

American family life and the world of the black church. Though the book was far from wholly positive about blacks and their lives, Baldwin was clear that he did not mean it to be a protest novel.

Another important writer of the period was a Chicago poet named Gwendolyn Brooks. Like Baldwin, Brooks did not shy away from racial issues. African American children, she wrote in

Ralph Ellison's 1952 novel *Invisible Man* describes the life of an unidentified black man who believes he is metaphorically invisible, which is partly due to race and partly to the human condition.

one poem, "are adjudged the leastwise in the land."[67] But Brooks rarely made race and racism the center of her work. In a series of poems published in 1949, for example, Brooks describes the life of Annie Allen, a young black woman. The poems are much more concerned with Allen's personal growth than with the unfairness of the world around her.

Perhaps the most famous writer of this era was a man named Ralph Ellison. Born in 1914, Ellison is best known today for his 1952 novel *Invisible Man*. This novel describes the life of a black man, never identified by name, who believes that he is metaphorically invisible—that is, the people around him never really notice him or care to learn much about him. The novel shows the narrator moving from a small town to an all-black college and on to New York City, where he looks for work and becomes involved in political activity.

In some ways *Invisible Man* reflects the themes of Wright's *Native Son* and *Black Boy*. Racism, for example, plays a major role in Ellison's novel. But *Invisible Man* also describes how other blacks fail the narrator. The African American college president sabotages the narrator's job search; the narrator's black political allies have no interest in getting to know him as a person. The narrator's feelings of invisibility, then, are partly due to his race—but in other ways, Ellison makes clear, these feelings are simply part of the human condition.

By the early 1950s, then, there were three important strands of African American literature: the assimilationist strand represented by writers such as Yerby, the deeply political strand represented by Wright, and the mix of the two represented by authors such as Baldwin, Brooks, and Ellison. As Baldwin's essay attacking Wright's fondness for protest novels shows, the writers associated with each strand did not always coexist comfortably. But those tensions did not last long. Beginning in the late 1950s, African American writers began to put aside their differences—and come together as never before.

Civil Rights

The catalyst for this change was political. In the late 1940s, tired of being mistreated, blacks across the South began to demand their civil rights—the basic rights, such as the right to vote, extended to all citizens of a nation. By the early 1950s the protesters had joined to form an organized movement. In the coming years, civil rights activists won many important victories. They convinced the U.S. Supreme Court to rule that segregation in school systems was against the law. They forced states to roll back laws that restricted the right of blacks to vote. And they helped pass the Civil Rights Act of 1964, which not only prohibited racial discrimination in public life but also gave the federal government the power to penalize those who continued to discriminate. Few social movements in American history have accomplished so much so quickly.

The movement also met with significant opposition, however, especially from white southerners. Some school districts shut down altogether rather than allow blacks and whites to share classrooms, and angry white adults taunted black children and threw rocks at them in several cities where desegregation took place. "Segregation now, segregation tomorrow, segregation forever,"[68] Alabama governor George Wallace promised his constituents in 1963. Many state and local governments did everything they could to prevent blacks from voting, regardless of the new laws. Police forces in a number of communities brutally attacked civil rights protesters. Some civil rights workers, among them black leader Martin Luther King Jr., paid for their activism with their lives.

The civil rights movement brought black people of all backgrounds together and gave them a shared experience, a shared goal, and a shared identity. Interest in black folklore and black history boomed, and activists looked to the past for strength and encouragement. Protesters sang spirituals as they marched for their rights; speakers quoted Frederick Douglass, W.E.B. DuBois, and earlier black thinkers.

Black writers responded accordingly. Between the late 1950s and the end of the 1960s, black literature became proudly and unreservedly about African Americans and their experience. Whether celebrating black history, publishing poems of protest, or writing novels of urban black life, the writers of the civil rights era focused on black culture and heritage and demanded rights for themselves and their people. More than ever before, African American writers were speaking with one voice.

Poet Gwendolyn Brooks's works were mostly about the black struggle for civil rights, including a haunting work on the murder of fourteen-year-old Emmett Till in Mississippi.

A New Focus

The civil rights movement had an impact on the way some veteran black writers thought about their work. Baldwin's *The Fire Next Time,* published in 1963, was one example. Though Baldwin had earlier complained about Richard Wright's perspective on race and race relations, *The Fire Next Time* represented a shift in his thinking. This book was an honest discussion of race in America—and an indictment of whites. "How can one respect, let alone adopt, the values of a people who do not, on any level whatever, live the way they say they do, or the way they say they should?"[69] Baldwin asked.

Much of Brooks's poetry from this period also deals explicitly with civil rights themes. One of her most haunting works fictionalizes the 1955 death of Emmett Till, a fourteen-year-old boy murdered by an angry mob in Mississippi after he supposedly whistled at a white woman. Brooks writes movingly of the teenager's "cramped cries" as he is taken prisoner, and describes the "gradual dulling of those Negro eyes"[70] as he is killed. Themes such as these were common in Brooks's work during this time.

The writers who most clearly reflected the literary themes of the time, however, were new writers who came of age during the tumultuous years of protest. Among the most important of these was a poet and playwright named LeRoi Jones, born in New Jersey in 1934. Jones was heavily influenced early in his writing career by young white poets who experimented with poetic styles and forms, and he moved easily within both black and white circles. By 1960 he seemed poised for a long and rewarding life at the cutting edge of the literary world.

In the early 1960s, however, Jones had a change of heart. Bemoaning the difficulties faced by civil rights protesters, Jones rejected white society and culture and took on an identity that was passionately African American. He began wearing African clothing and changed his name to Imamu Amiri Baraka. Baraka's poetry became highly political, often militant, and it urged blacks of all nations to band together. "Black people, come in, wherever you are," he wrote in his poem "SOS," "urgent, calling you, calling all black people."[71]

By the mid-1960s Baraka's writing had become a ferocious indictment of the American system. His poems, plays, and prose attacked the United States, white Americans—whether they supported the civil rights movement or not—and blacks who Baraka believed were not radical enough. As Baraka wrote in an essay, the civil rights struggle was not about "the survival of this society, this filthy order." It was about making sweeping changes in the status of black people—and making these changes in any way necessary. "The hope is that young blacks will remember all their lives [the injustices] they are seeing," he wrote, "and that eventually they will . . . erupt like Mt. Vesuvius [a volcano] to crush in hot lava those willful maniacs who call themselves white Americans."[72]

Martin Luther King Jr. and Malcolm X

Several leaders of the civil rights movement made invaluable contributions to African American literature. *Letter from Birmingham Jail*, written by Martin Luther King Jr. after he was arrested during a 1963 protest march, describes many of King's core principles in clear yet eloquent language. King's "I Have a Dream" speech, given at the Lincoln Memorial later in 1963, is even better known. In this speech King describes his vision for an America in which skin color and ethnic heritage do not matter, an America in which all people are able to enjoy the same rights and freedoms regardless of their heritage. The "I Have a Dream" speech ranks among the most famous pieces of writing in all American history.

Another important leader, Malcolm X, also added to the writings that sprang from the civil rights movement. More radical than King, Malcolm was a Muslim whose message appealed particularly to poor urban black men with little education and less hope. Malcolm's speeches and writings reflected his image of black America—an image often at odds with King's vision. In particular, where King was ever hopeful that integration would

be a success, Malcolm was much less optimistic. "You can sometimes be 'with' whites," he told American blacks, "but never 'of' them." Like the best of King's works, Malcolm's autobiography has long been acknowledged for its literary as well as its political merit.

Quoted in *Time*. "Malcolm X: History as Hope." February 23, 1970. www.time.com/time/magazine/article/0,9171,876659,00.html.

Though Martin Luther King Jr., left, and Malcolm X had their differences on the course of the civil rights movement, they both made invaluable contributions to African American literature.

Politics, History, and Daily Life

Many other black writers of the civil rights era followed Baraka's lead by producing deeply political works, though usually of a more subtle nature. Lorraine Hansberry's play *A Raisin in the Sun* is one example. It demonstrates the connection of politics and literature in this era. The play, dating from 1959, was the first drama written by an African American woman to be produced on Broadway. *A Raisin in the Sun* is about a black Chicago family's attempts to navigate an often-hostile world. When the family buys a house in an all-white neighborhood, for example, their prospective neighbors try to keep them from moving in. *A Raisin in the Sun* has a positive ending—family members continue to pursue their dreams despite the obstacles—but prejudice is ever-present in the play.

Some African American writings of the period were less overtly political. Still, they echoed the political changes in America by celebrating black life and taking pride in their race. "I am a black woman," wrote poet Mari Evans in 1969, "tall as a cypress/strong . . . Look/on me and be/renewed."[73] Other writers explored African American history. "Black is a boy who knows his heroes,"[74] wrote James Emanuel in a poem that discussed some important black figures of the past. As the new generation of writers saw it, African Americans of the 1960s needed to understand the history of their people in order to make their way in the world.

Still other writers concentrated on describing the lives of ordinary black people. While racial discrimination was present in most of these works, and black history often played a role as well, the emphasis in these works tended to be on individuals: their work, their play, and their families. Ernest J. Gaines, for example, wrote about life in rural Louisiana in books such as *Bloodline* and *Of Love and Dust*, both published in the late 1960s. Paule Marshall, the Brooklyn-born daughter of parents from Barbados, described the lives of Caribbean immigrants in her coming-of-age novel *Brown Girl, Brownstones*. Books that focused on individuals and family life had been part of the Harlem Renaissance, to be sure, but during the civil rights era the number of novels on this theme mushroomed.

Alex Haley

Born in 1921 in Ithaca, New York, Alex Haley produced important works both during the civil rights era and afterward. In the early 1960s, while working as a journalist, Haley frequently interviewed civil rights leader Malcolm X. Before long Haley and Malcolm decided to turn these interviews into a full-length book. Though the finished product was called *The Autobiography of Malcolm X*, it was a joint effort from the beginning, and Haley received full credit for his part in the work. The book was published in 1965, shortly after Malcolm was assassinated, and was a popular and critical success.

Haley is probably more famous today, however, for a book he published in 1976, more than ten years after the appearance of *The Autobiography of Malcolm X*. This new book was called *Roots: The Saga of an American Family*. Partly fictionalized but generally based on fact, the book took the reader through seven generations of Haley's family history, beginning

with an ancestor who was born in Africa and brought to North America as a slave. The following year *Roots* was made into a wildly successful television miniseries. Together the book and the miniseries sparked an enormous interest in genealogy and history, particularly among African Americans.

Alex Haley published his best-selling novel *Roots* in 1976. The book was made into an award-winning TV miniseries, and together they sparked Americans' interest in their own genealogical roots.

In many ways the writings of the civil rights movement are as different from one another as the works of the Harlem Renaissance. There is a large gap in tone between the uncompromising rhetoric of Baraka's essays, for example, and the much more subtle poetry of Brooks. Evans's proud declaration of blackness contrasts with the struggles of Marshall's Barbadian immigrants to come to terms with what it means to be black in a new land.

Yet at heart the works of the civil rights era show a remarkable consistency. After a decade or two in which African American writers drifted in different directions, the civil rights movement unified them again. The political struggles of the time forced black writers to confront the reality that they were black in a society built and run largely by whites. As a result, the writings of the civil rights era were overtly political in a way that was not true of the colonial period, the Harlem Renaissance, or most other periods in African American literature. By reinforcing the message of the protest movement, the literature of the civil rights era ultimately helped to change the status of blacks in the American South.

The African American authors of the late 1950s and the 1960s differed when it came to style, tone, and genre. But each poet, playwright, and novelist of the period addressed the same basic theme in his or her writing: what it was like to be black in a white world. Honest, unflinching, and deeply evocative of America during the civil rights years, the writing of the period is of historic importance—and of exceptional literary value as well.

Chapter Six

Into a New Century: 1970–Present

Artistic styles and fashions are often easy to associate with a particular time and place. The music of Johann Sebastian Bach, for example, has a distinctive sound that makes it clearly a product of Europe in the early 1700s, and the paintings of Claude Monet show techniques common to French artists in the years around 1900. African American literature is no exception. The period after the Civil War saw a rise in fiction and poetry written by blacks, while the civil rights era was known for the many poems, essays, and novels that attacked racism and stressed black pride. In the same way, slave narratives and abolitionist essays characterized the literature of the 1850s.

Since the end of the 1960s, however, African American literature has become increasingly diverse—and increasingly difficult to classify. No single characteristic defines black writing during these decades. Black writers of the present day have a variety of styles, forms, genres, and influences at their disposal—and make excellent use of all of them. The result is a rich mixture of writings that ranges from rap lyrics to experimental poetry and from memoirs to dramas. For this reason, the modern age is in some ways the most fascinating in the history of black literature.

Maya Angelou

There have been quite a few important black writers during recent times. Of these men and women, though, one stands out for the length and breadth of her career and the enormous influence she has had on other writers. This author, Maya Angelou, has done as much as anyone to create the modern era of African American literature—and ranks as perhaps the most significant writer of the last several decades.

Born in Missouri in 1928, Angelou has had a long and extremely varied career, not all of it focused on literature. As a young adult she was active in the civil rights movement, for example, and Angelou has been a college professor as well as an actor, dancer, and film director. Still, she is best known for her writing, most notably for her poetry. In 1993 she attracted national attention by reading her poem "On the Pulse of Morning" at the inauguration of President Bill Clinton, and she remains one of America's best-selling poets.

Although poetry has made Angelou famous, critics admire her more for a series of memoirs. The first of these books, *I Know Why the Caged Bird Sings*, follows Angelou from early childhood to high school graduation. Emotionally intense and written in a style more reminiscent of a novel than a standard autobiography, *I Know Why the Caged Bird Sings* was an immediate success upon its publication in 1969. Critics praised Angelou's use of language, her ability to evoke the rural South of her childhood, and her sensitive handling of difficult topics. "Maya Angelou writes like a song," one reviewer wrote, "and like the truth."[75]

The subject matter of *I Know Why the Caged Bird Sings* was certainly compelling. The book tells of Angelou's abandonment by both parents at an early age, describes the constant racism she experienced growing up in a small Arkansas town, and reveals that she was raped as a girl by her mother's boyfriend. Despite the grim subject matter, though, the book also has many uplifting passages. At one point, for example, Angelou learns the power of spoken words when an adult reads to her from a novel. "I heard poetry for the first time in my life," Angelou writes. "Her voice

Maya Angelou is perhaps the most significant African American author in the past few decades. Here, as the poet laureate of the United States, she reads one of her poems at President Bill Clinton's inauguration in 1993.

slid in and curved down through and over the words. She was nearly singing. . . . Her reading was a wonder in my ears."[76]

The success of *I Know Why the Caged Bird Sings* and the other memoirs that followed it encouraged other American writers to publish memoirs of their own. Many of these writers, moreover, were deeply influenced by the artistry of Angelou's language and the novel-like narrative techniques she used in her works. Indeed,

Angelou's book *I Know Why the Caged Bird Sings* was a memoir not only about growing up black in America but also about growing up female and confronting numerous prejudices.

so many subsequent memoirs were modeled after Angelou's that some critics argue that Angelou invented the modern American autobiography.

Angelou and Feminism

Angelou is probably best known today, however, for her inclusion of feminist ideas in her work. Feminism is a social movement that gained prominence in the 1960s and 1970s as activists sought to improve the lives of women. Besides tearing down the barriers that kept women from achieving full equality with men, feminists also hoped to validate the experience of being female. Women's perspectives were too often ignored, feminists argued, and as a result many women believed that their experiences did not matter or were somehow not quite real. To combat this perception, feminist leaders encouraged women to share the stories of their lives as women. Their goal was twofold: to help women reclaim their voices and to help them realize that their perspective was both important and true.

In the beginning, feminism was primarily a movement of well-educated, upper-middle-class white women. By the late 1960s, though, it was beginning to have a significant impact on black women as well. *I Know Why the Caged Bird Sings* was among the first books by an African American to express a feminist sensibility. Angelou's memoir is not simply about growing up black in America; rather, it is about growing up both black and female. Black women, Angelou writes, are trapped in the "crossfire of masculine prejudice, white illogical hate and Black lack of power."[77]

The success of *I Know Why the Caged Bird Sings* helped turn conventional publishing wisdom on its head. For years, publishers had put their resources into marketing books by male authors such as Richard Wright and Ralph Ellison, and devoted less energy and money to women's writings. Angelou's work, however, proved as popular as anything written by a black man, and publishers took notice. *I Know Why the Caged Bird Sings* helped usher in an era of new opportunities for black female writers.

Alice Walker

Indeed, the years since 1970 in African American literature have been especially notable for the number of great women writers.

Among the most prominent of these is Alice Walker. Born in 1944, Walker grew up in Georgia when segregation was still in force. From very early on, she impressed people with her intelligence and curiosity. "She could outspell children twice her age," recalls her first teacher. "A lot of children passed my way, but Alice Walker was the smartest one I ever had."[78]

During and after college, Walker was active in both the women's rights and civil rights movements. Both movements influenced Walker's writing. The connections are easy to see in Walker's first novel, *The Third Life of Grange Copeland*, which was published in 1970. The main character, Grange Copeland, is a poor black farmer who is repeatedly mocked and harassed by a white man. Copeland deals with his frustrations by beating his wife. When Copeland's son grows up and marries, he treats his own wife the same way. "It was his rage at himself, and his life and his world that made him beat her," Walker writes of the son. "His rage could and did blame everything, *everything* on her."[79] When whites oppress and belittle African American men, Walker is saying, African American women suffer too.

Walker's best-known novel today is *The Color Purple,* which appeared in 1982 and was later made into a successful movie featuring Whoopi Goldberg and Oprah Winfrey. As a young teenager, the main character, Celie, is raped by her father, forced to give up two children for adoption, and beaten by her husband. At one point in the novel she feels abandoned even by God. "The God I been praying and writing to is a man," she tells a friend. "And act just like all the other mens I know. Trifling, forgitful, and lowdown."[80] However, things ultimately improve for Celie. She is finally able to stand up to her husband and make a new and more successful life for herself.

Toni Morrison

Toni Morrison, born in Ohio in 1931, was another female writer who helped make the experiences of African American women an important and essential part of black literature. Morrison published her first novel, *The Bluest Eye*, in 1970. Like the works of Walker and Angelou, *The Bluest Eye* focuses on the impact of racial issues on African American girls and women. The title of the novel comes from the wish of one of the characters, a black girl,

The Color Purple

———————◆———————

Alice Walker's novel *The Color Purple* has been widely praised for its realism, its vivid characters, and its tale of a young woman who manages to overcome the tragedies of her life. One of the most enthusiastic assessments of the novel comes from Peter S. Prescott, a book critic who served as a judge on the panel that awarded *The Color Purple* the Pulitzer Prize for Fiction in 1983.

> There were strong books [that year], . . . But nothing appeared that could best the Walker novel for the Pulitzer Prize. In that realm, Alice Walker had no competition. Over time, *The Color Purple* has achieved a status few books ever attain. It is one of the few books that is read by most students in the country. It has become a rite of passage.

> It is also one of the few literary books to capture the popular imagination and leave a permanent imprint on our society. There are some commercial books that did that, like *The Godfather* [a 1969 novel by Mario Puzo, later turned into a movie]. . . . But *The Color Purple* is literature of the highest form. If an author has anything to show you, she'll show you on the first page. Alice Walker met the mark and then continued to soar. . . . I fulfilled my duty, as charged, to find the most distinguished American novel. In that sense, I am proud to be a part of history.

Quoted in Evelyn C. White. *Alice Walker*. New York: Norton, 2004, pp. 356–357.

Alice Walker's Pulitzer Prize–winning novel *The Color Purple* is now read by a large portion of students in the United States.

to have blue eyes—a painful indication that she would prefer not to be African American.

The Bluest Eye was a success both financially and critically. However, Morrison is best known today for two later novels: *Song of Solomon*, published in 1977, and 1988's *Beloved*. Both novels are based on themes from black history and folklore. *Song of Solomon* springs from a legend that a group of slaves once sprouted wings and flew back to Africa. *Beloved* is based on the true story

Toni Morrison won the Pulitzer Prize for Fiction for her novel *Beloved*. It is based on the true story of runaway slave Margaret Garner.

of fugitive slave Margaret Garner. Both novels were popular with critics as well as with the general public; *Beloved* won the Pulitzer Prize for Fiction, and in 2006 a group of critics voted it the best American novel since 1980. Both novels have also been widely praised for the beauty of the writing as well as for the significance of the messages the books contain. For Morrison, each aspect of her writing is equally important. "The best art is political," she argues, "and irrevocably beautiful at the same time."[81]

The success of Angelou, Walker, and Morrison has had an obvious impact on other African American women writers. From folklorist and novelist Virginia Hamilton to poet Rita Dove, many black women have risen to prominence in the literary world in part because of the works of these three pioneering women. But Angelou, Walker, and Morrison have helped to bring male African American writers to the public's attention as well. At no other point in African American history have books by black authors sold as well as they sell in modern times; at no other point have African American writers, male or female, received the critical acclaim that they do today.

Traditional Forms and Styles

Many themes used by African American writers of today reflect themes common in earlier eras of black literature. The lives of ordinary black people, the struggles of black immigrants—these and other themes appear frequently in the works of modern African American authors, just as they did in the works of the post–Civil War period or the Harlem Renaissance. One example is the work of playwright August Wilson. Born in Pittsburgh in 1945, Wilson is best known today for a series of plays about black life in Pittsburgh during the 1900s. Two of these plays, *Fences* and *The Piano Lesson*, won the Pulitzer Prize for Drama. Like earlier writers, such as Langston Hughes and Lorraine Hansberry, Wilson was noted for his ability to write honestly and accurately about the lives of ordinary African Americans. One critic wrote that watching a Wilson play was "like eavesdropping on a group of family members."[82]

Still other writers followed the lead of authors such as Richard Wright, who had written unflinchingly of life among the poorest of African Americans. An author known as Sapphire, for example,

Young Adult Fiction

As is true of mysteries, romance novels, and other types of genre fiction, the market for young adult books has boomed since the 1980s. Virginia Hamilton, a writer from Ohio, was one of the first black novelists to earn success in this field. Before her death in 2002, Hamilton published several well-received books of folklore, including *The People Could Fly* and *Her Stories*, aimed primarily at young people. She is also known for her young adult fiction, notably her novels *Zeely* and *The House of Dies Drear,* along with *M.C. Higgins, the Great*, which won the Newbery Award as the best children's novel of 1975. Though Hamilton's folklore looks to the past, her novels are most often set in contemporary times.

Mildred Taylor is another modern author who is best known for her work for young people. Her work, more than Hamilton's, focuses on African American history; her novels *Roll of Thunder, Hear My Cry* and *Let the Circle Be Unbroken* each describes what life was like for Southern blacks during the years immediately after the Civil War. Both of these novels won awards and remain widely read today. Taylor has also written books set in the pre–Civil War South.

Two African American men have also written extensively for young adults. One, Walter Dean Myers, writes most often of children growing up in Harlem during the present day. His novels deal with controversial topics such as drug abuse and gang violence. One of his best-known works to date is *Scorpions*, which was nominated for a Newbery Award in 1989. More recently, Christopher Paul Curtis has won awards for historical novels such as *Bud, Not Buddy*—set in Michigan during the 1930s—and *The Watsons Go to Birmingham, 1963*, which deals with a Northern black family's arrival in Alabama at a critical point in the civil rights movement.

Children's fiction writer Virginia Hamilton's novels often mix folklore of the past with contemporary settings.

published a novel called *Push* in 1996. Though the subject matter was distressing—the novel dealt with themes such as illiteracy, incest, and abuse—the book sold extremely well. In 2009, the novel was made into a successful movie called *Precious*.

A final example is the theme of immigration. From Phillis Wheatley to Claude McKay, many great black writers over the years have been immigrants. Among black immigrant writers today, Edwidge Danticat and Jamaica Kincaid stand out. Both of these women were born in the Caribbean and came to the United States as teenagers. Danticat's *Breath, Eyes, Memory*, published in 1994, and Kincaid's *Annie John*, which appeared in 1985, describe the challenges faced by newcomers to the United States.

Genre Fiction, Dance, and Rhythm

The modern era has seen remarkable growth in genre fiction— that is, fiction that fits under headings such as romance, science fiction, and mystery. For many years, black writers were not typically involved in these branches of publishing. Even today, most authors of genre fiction are white. But the number of African Americans recognized for their contributions to these fields is growing steadily.

Octavia Butler, for example, is a noted science fiction and fantasy writer. Born in 1947 in California, Butler was drawn to science fiction as a girl. She has published a series of novels that deals with a four-thousand-year-old being named Doro; these books have sold well among African Americans and among fans of science fiction in general. Butler's most familiar work is probably a time-travel novel called *Kindred*, which she published in 1988. This book tells of a young black woman of the present day who suddenly finds herself on a southern plantation before the Civil War.

Several African American writers have produced successful mystery novels as well. The best known of these writers is Walter Mosley. Born in Michigan in 1952, Mosley has written a number of books about a private detective named Easy Rawlins. Rawlins, a veteran of World War II, solves crimes in Los Angeles. Though some critics look down on mystery fiction and other genre books, Mosley defends his work. "The mystery genre is there to help us deal with what's going on in our world socially and politically," Mosley says. "Literature helps in many ways by talking about this."[83]

Octavia Butler is an award-winning science-fiction and fantasy writer whose novel *Kindred* is about a contemporary black girl who is suddenly transported to a southern plantation before the Civil War.

The modern era in African American literature also includes a new focus on the combination of writing with other art forms. One of the most important of these writers is Ntozake Shange, born in New Jersey in 1948. Several of Shange's works combine poetry, music, and dance into one dramatic composition. Performers dance and recite the words to poems on a stage devoid of sets, props, or backdrops. Shange is best known today for a work with the title *for colored girls who have considered suicide/when the rainbow is enuf.* The work is meant to be performed by seven women, each dressed in a different color.

Other black writers of the modern age are likewise concerned with more than just words. Gil Scott-Heron, born in Chicago in 1949, is best remembered today for his poem "The Revolution Will Not Be Televised," which he often performed to the rhythm of drumbeats—a style that influenced the rap and hip-hop movements of today. This poem contains references to politicians and celebrities of the time, along with advertising slogans and commercial products. Scott-Heron's point was that television and other forms of entertainment were distractions for black people that focused their attention away from the inequalities in the United States. "The revolution will not be brought to you by Xerox," reads one line, and the poem concludes, "The revolution will be live."[84]

Literature Through the Years

African American literature has changed considerably in the years since the first black people arrived in North America. Styles have changed and so have themes. The high-flown poetry of Wheatley has given way to the unrhymed free verse of Hughes; the narratives of escaped slaves have been replaced by the memoirs of Angelou. With few exceptions, black writers were ignored until long past the Civil War; today, authors such as Morrison win major prizes and awards. In some ways, it is hard to see much commonality between the generations in black literature.

But three themes have been constant. The first is that each succeeding generation of African American writers has inched closer toward the mainstream of American literature. This progress parallels the social and political movement of African Americans toward ever greater tolerance and even acceptance. More and more,

Americans think of black authors not simply as African Americans writers, but as American writers. Years ago, books by blacks were shunted to the side and ignored by the white majority—if indeed they were published at all. Today, the world is different.

A second common theme is that nearly every African American writer through the years has dealt in some way with the question of what it means to be black in a white-dominated society. Some authors have described being African American as a burden. Others have seen it as a source of pride. Many have described it as both positive and negative, a curse and a blessing. From the "black and unknown bards"[85] who wrote the spirituals to the best-selling

Rap, Hip-Hop, and More

Literary critics once looked down on song lyrics, which they saw as something less than true literature. Today, however, that scorn is much less widespread: Song lyrics are increasingly viewed as a form of poetry and a literary genre, studied in university courses and analyzed by scholars. Modern African American writers, accordingly, have made names for themselves as lyricists.

Some of the most famous of these songwriters work in the field of rap music. Big Daddy Kane, born in 1968, is widely admired not only as a fine performer, but as an excellent writer of rap lyrics as well. "Kane is one of the most incredible lyricists," says fellow rap star Ice-T. Other rap lyricists of note include Lil Wayne, born in 1979, and LL Cool J, whose lyrics often have a romantic quality unusual in the rap world.

Still other African Americans are achieving success writing lyrics for other genres. Mary J. Blige and will.i.am (real name William Adams), for example, have written pop and hip-hop lyrics as well as the words to rap songs. Alice Randall, a novelist and professor who was born in 1959, has written the lyrics for many successful country songs; she collaborated with another writer to produce the 1994 hit "XXXs and OOOs," which reached the top of the country music chart for singer Trisha Yearwood. And singer CeCe Winans, born in 1964, has written a number of popular gospel songs.

Quoted in MTV.com. "The Greatest MCs of All Time." www.mtv.com/bands/h/hip_hop_week/2006/emcees/index5.jhtml.

novelists of the present day, an awareness of race has rarely been far from the surface in the works of black authors.

Finally, whether publishing science fiction or writing impassioned attacks on racism, whether composing sonnets or retelling folklore, black writers have always drawn inspiration from those who came before them. The title of Angelou's memoir *I Know Why the Caged Bird Sings* comes from a poem by nineteenth-century poet Paul Laurence Dunbar. Morrison, Charles Chesnutt, and Zora Neale Hurston, among many others, used images and stories from black folklore in their works. And references to the spirituals abound in black stories, poetry, and nonfiction, from the title of James Baldwin's novel *Go Tell It on the Mountain* to the closing lines of Martin Luther King's "I Have a Dream" speech: "Thank God almighty, I'm free at last."[86] In every era, the works of black writers helped set the stage for the achievements of the next generation. Whatever the future may bring for African American literature, the writers who come along next will surely be influenced by the authors who came before them.

Notes

Chapter One: The Oral Tradition and the First Black Writers: 1600–1820

1. Roger D. Abrahams. *Afro-American Folktales*. New York: Pantheon, 1985, p. 4.

2. Joel Chandler Harris. *Uncle Remus*. New York: George Routledge and Sons, 1883, p. 18.

3. Quoted in Hurston. *Every Tongue Got to Confess*. New York: Harper-Collins, 2001, p. 91.

4. Quoted in William Francis Allen, Charles Pickard Ware, and Lucy McKim Garrison. *Slave Songs of the United States*. Bedford, MA: Apple-wood, n.d., p. 99.

5. Quoted in Timothy Earl Fulop and Albert J. Raboteau. *African-American Religion*. New York: Taylor and Francis, 1996, p. 80.

6. Quoted in Daryl Cumber Dance. *From My People: 400 Years of African American Folklore*. New York: Norton, 2002, p. 84.

7. Quoted in Dance. *From My People: 400 Years of African American Folklore*, p. 79.

8. Quoted in Kai Wright, ed. *The African American Experience: Black History and Culture Through Speeches, Letters, Editorials, Poems, Songs, and Stories*. New York: Black Dog & Leventhal, 2009, p. 58.

9. Quoted in Vincent L. Wimbush and Rosamond C. Rodman. *African Americans and the Bible: Sacred Texts and Social Textures*. New York: Continuum, 2000, p. 236.

10. Quoted in Faith Berry. *From Bondage to Liberation*. New York: Continuum, 1996, p. 14.

11. Quoted in Richard Barksdale and Keneth Kinnamon, eds. *Black Writers of America: A Comprehensive Anthology*. New York: Macmillan, 1972, p. 43.

12. Barksdale and Kinnamon, eds. *Black Writers of America: A Comprehensive Anthology*, pp. 39–40.

13. Quoted in Barksdale and Kinnamon, eds. *Black Writers of America: A Comprehensive Anthology*, p. 41.

14. Quoted in Dudley Randall, ed. *The Black Poets*. New York: Bantam Books, 1970, p. 37.

15. Arna Bontemps, ed. *Great Slave Narratives*. Boston: Beacon, 1969, p. xii.

Chapter Two: Slave and Free: 1800–1865

16. David Walker. *Appeal to the Coloured Citizens of the World*. Reprint, Univer-

sity Park: Pennsylvania State University Press, 2000, p. 76.

17. Walker. *Appeal to the Coloured Citizens of the World*, p. 42.

18. Quoted in Barksdale and Kinnamon, eds. *Black Writers of America: A Comprehensive Anthology*, p. 177.

19. Quoted in Henry Louis Gates Jr. and Nellie Y. McKay, eds. *African American Literature: The Norton Anthology*. New York: Norton, 1997, p. 414.

20. Quoted in Barksdale and Kinnamon, eds. *Black Writers of America: A Comprehensive Anthology*, p. 192.

21. Quoted in Barksdale and Kinnamon, eds. *Black Writers of America: A Comprehensive Anthology*, p. 216.

22. Quoted in Bontemps, ed. *Great Slave Narratives*, p. 218.

23. Quoted in Bontemps, ed. *Great Slave Narratives*, p. 103.

24. William and Ellen Craft. *Running a Thousand Miles for Freedom*. Gloucester, UK: Dodo Press, n.d., p. 79.

25. Henry Brown. *Narrative of Henry Box Brown*. Boston: Brown and Stearns, 1849, p. 61.

26. Frederick Douglass. *Narrative of the Life of Frederick Douglass*. Boston: Anti-Slavery Office, 1847, p. 101.

27. Douglass. *Narrative of the Life of Frederick Douglass*, p. 81.

28. Quoted in Barksdale and Kinnamon, eds. *Black Writers of America: A Comprehensive Anthology*, p. 68.

Chapter Three: After the Civil War: 1865–1918

29. Quoted in Barksdale and Kinnamon, eds. *Black Writers of America: A Comprehensive Anthology*, p. 326.

30. Quoted in Gates and McKay, eds. *African American Literature: The Norton Anthology*, p. 538.

31. Quoted in Houston A. Baker Jr. *Black Literature in America*. New York: McGraw-Hill, 1971, p. 114.

32. Quoted in Gates and McKay, eds. *African American Literature: The Norton Anthology*, p. 896.

33. Quoted in Barksdale and Kinnamon, eds. *Black Writers of America: A Comprehensive Anthology*, p. 352.

34. Quoted in Gates and McKay, eds. *African American Literature: The Norton Anthology*, p. 769.

35. Quoted in The Episcopal Church. *The Hymnal 1982*. New York: Church Pension Fund, 1985, unpaginated (Hymn #599).

36. "Negro National Anthem." Oxford African American Studies Center. www.oxfordaasc.com/article/aag/894.

37. Booker T. Washington. *Up from Slavery*. 1901. Reprint, New York: Penguin, 1986, p. xii.

38. Washington. *Up from Slavery*, p. 21.

39. Washington. *Up from Slavery,* pp. 235–236.

40. Quoted in Baker. *Black Literature in America,* p. 105.

41. W.E. Burghardt DuBois. "Strivings of the Negro People," *The Atlantic.* August 1897. www.theatlantic.com/past/docs/unbound/flashbks/black/dubstriv.htm.

Chapter Four: The Harlem Renaissance: 1918–1940

42. Quoted in Glenn Stout. *Young Woman and the Sea.* New York: Houghton Mifflin Harcourt, 2009, p. 219.

43. Quoted in William S. McConnell. *Harlem Renaissance.* San Diego: Greenhaven, 2003, p. 24.

44. Quoted in Valerie Boyd. *Wrapped in Rainbows.* New York: Scribner, 2002, p. 93.

45. Quoted in Boyd. *Wrapped in Rainbows,* p. 90.

46. Quoted in Randall, ed. *The Black Poets,* p. 100.

47. Quoted in Cary D. Wintz. *Harlem Speaks.* Naperville, IL: Sourcebooks, 2007, p. 72.

48. Quoted in Gates and McKay, eds. *African American Literature: The Norton Anthology,* p. 1254.

49. Zora Neale Hurston. *Their Eyes Were Watching God.* 1937. Reprint, New York: HarperCollins, 2006, p. 38.

50. Quoted in Baker. *Black Literature in America,* p. 166.

51. Quoted in Barksdale and Kinnamon, eds. *Black Writers of America: A Comprehensive Anthology,* p. 519.

52. Quoted in Akida Sullivan Harper. *Langston Hughes: Short Stories.* New York: Hill and Wang, 1996, p. 41.

53. Quoted in Barksdale and Kinnamon, eds. *Black Writers of America: A Comprehensive Anthology,* p. 519.

54. Nella Larsen. *Passing.* New York: Collier Books, 1971, p. 123.

55. Zora Neale Hurston. *The Complete Stories.* New York: HarperCollins, 1995, p. 25.

56. Quoted in Randall, ed. *The Black Poets,* p. 95.

57. Quoted in McConnell. *Harlem Renaissance,* p. 48.

58. *Mason City (IA) Globe-Gazette.* "Scanning New Books," February 23, 1929, p. 4.

59. Quoted in Wintz. *Harlem Speaks,* p. 15.

60. Quoted in Valerie Boyd. "Zora Neale Hurston." www.zoranealehurston.com/books/their_eyes_ps.html.

61. Quoted in Barksdale and Kinnamon, eds. *Black Writers of America: A Comprehensive Anthology,* p. 475.

62. Quoted in Wintz. *Harlem Speaks,* p. 15.

Chapter Five: Through the Civil Rights Struggle: 1940–1969

63. Quoted in Barksdale and Kinnamon, eds. *Black Writers of America: A Comprehensive Anthology,* p. 655.

64. Quoted in Jerry H. Bryant. *Born in a Mighty Bad Land: The Violent Man in*

African American Folklore and Fiction. Bloomington: Indiana University Press, 2003, p. 4.

65. *Time.* "Books: Bad N—". March 4, 1940. www.time.com/time/magazine/article/0,9171,763619,00.html?internalid=atb100.

66. Quoted in Barksdale and Kinnamon, eds. *Black Writers of America: A Comprehensive Anthology*, p. 547.

67. Quoted in Randall, ed. *The Black Poets*, p. 166.

68. Quoted in Dan T. Carter. *The Politics of Rage.* New York: Simon and Schuster, 1995, p. 11.

69. James Baldwin. *The Fire Next Time.* New York: Dial, 1963, p. 96.

70. Quoted in Baker. *Black Literature in America*, p. 333.

71. Quoted in Randall, ed. *The Black Poets*, p. 181.

72. Quoted in Barksdale and Kinnamon, eds. *Black Writers of America: A Comprehensive Anthology*, p. 758.

73. Quoted in Baker. *Black Literature in America*, p. 350.

74. Quoted in Randall, ed. *The Black Poets*, p. 190.

Chapter Six: Into a New Century: 1970–Present

75. Quoted in Annie Gottlieb. "Angelou," in *Contemporary Authors.* Detroit: Gale, 1987, p. 23.

76. Maya Angelou. *I Know Why the Caged Bird Sings.* New York: Random House, 1969, p. 97.

77. Angelou. *I Know Why the Caged Bird Sings*, p. 265.

78. Quoted in Evelyn C. White. *Alice Walker.* New York: Norton, 2004, p. 15.

79. Quoted in White. *Alice Walker*, p. 186.

80. Quoted in Gates and McKay, eds. *African American Literature: The Norton Anthology*, p. 2406.

81. Quoted in Mari Evans, ed. *Black Women Writers, 1950–1980.* Garden City, NY: Anchor Doubleday, 1984, p. 345.

82. Quoted in Gates and McKay, eds. *African American Literature: The Norton Anthology*, p. 2411.

83. Quoted in *Wall Street Journal.* "Mosley Speaks." www.crimetime.co.uk/mag/index.php/showarticle/769.

84. Gil Scott-Heron. "The Revolution Will Not Be Televised." www.gilscottheron.com/lyrevol.html.

85. Quoted in Gates and McKay, eds. *African American Literature: The Norton Anthology*, p. 769.

86. Quoted in Dorothy Cotton. "I Remember Martin," *Ebony*, April 1984, p. 34.

Glossary

abolitionism: A nineteenth-century movement to eliminate slavery in the United States.

civil rights: The rights and privileges extended to people simply by virtue of being citizens.

folklore: The stories, songs, and other forms of literature developed by a culture.

genre: A type of literature, such as poetry, drama, or biography.

ghostwriters: People who actually write books that are published under someone else's name; often used when the supposed author is a celebrity.

Harlem Renaissance: A literary movement centering on the New York City community of Harlem in the 1920s.

literacy: The ability to read and write.

memoirs: Autobiographical accounts.

metaphors: Literary devices in which one object or idea is used to represent another, such as calling imagination an "imperial queen."

oral tradition: The communication of folklore from one person to another.

prose: Any form of writing other than poetry.

protest novel: A book of fiction that attacks a problem in society.

satire: A piece of literature that mocks or makes fun of human error or ignorance.

segregation: The separation of people according to race or other characteristics.

slave narrative: An account of life in slavery and subsequent escape, written or told by a former slave.

spirituals: Religious songs created by African Americans in the years before the Civil War.

For More Information

Books

Maya Angelou. *I Know Why the Caged Bird Sings.* New York: Random House, 1969. A groundbreaking autobiographical account of growing up in the rural South during segregation and one of the first African American books to show the influence of the feminist movement.

Stephen Currie. *African American Folklore.* Detroit: Lucent, 2009. Information about the folk traditions of black America.

Daryl Cumber Dance. *From My People: 400 Years of African American Folklore.* New York: Norton, 2002. An outstanding volume of traditional folk materials from African America. Includes the words to spirituals and blues songs as well as traditional folktales.

Henry Louis Gates Jr. and Evelyn Brooks Higginbotham. *Harlem Renaissance: Lives from the African American National Biography.* New York: Oxford University Press, 2009. Biographical sketches of authors involved in the Harlem Renaissance, along with background material on the movement.

Henry Louis Gates Jr. and Nellie Y. McKay. *African American Literature: The Norton Anthology.* New York: Norton, 1997. A vast anthology of black writings from colonial times to the end of the twentieth century. Includes extensive notes on the writers and suggestions for further research.

Dudley Randall. *The Black Poets.* New York: Bantam Books, 1970. A useful collection of poems by African American authors, with a particular emphasis on the writers of the Harlem Renaissance and the civil rights movement.

Amy Sickels. *African American Writers.* New York: Chelsea House, 2010. A survey of important black writers and their works.

Alice Walker. *The Color Purple.* New York: Harcourt Brace Jovanovich, 1992. Walker's best-known novel, widely acknowledged as one of the finest pieces of writing ever to appear in the United States.

Booker T. Washington. *Up from Slavery.* 1901. Reprint, New York: Penguin, 1986. A compelling and influential account of Washington's life and work.

Tyrone Williams, ed. *Masterplots II: African American Literature.* Pasadena, CA: Salem, 2009. A sourcebook that includes information on famous literary works written by blacks and information on the authors of those works as well.

Cary D. Wintz. *Harlem Speaks.* Naperville, IL: Sourcebooks, 2007. A thorough account of the Harlem

Renaissance, focusing on literature but including information on music, dance, and the visual arts as well. Includes a companion CD.

Kai Wright, ed. *The African American Experience.* New York: Black Dog and Leventhal, 2009. Poems, stories, speeches, and other important writings that helped shape African America today.

Websites

Academy of American Poets (www .poets.org/index.php). Links to poems and biographies of influential poets throughout history, including many African Americans.

New York Public Library, "African American Women Writers of the Nineteenth Century" (http://digital. nypl.org/schomburg/writers_aa19/toc.

html). Includes poetry, fiction, and other works written by black women in the 1800s.

PBS, "Slave Narratives and Uncle Tom's Cabin" (www.pbs.org/wgbh/aia/ part4/4p2958.html). Information on slave narratives, with links to further information related to African American literature.

Frederick Douglass.org, "Three Speeches by Frederick Douglass" (www .frederickdouglass.org/speeches/index. html). The complete texts of three of Douglass's most famous speeches; the site links to a biography of Douglass and other information as well.

Zora Neale Hurston (http://zoraneale hurston.com/). Information and links about the Harlem Renaissance figure best known for writing *Their Eyes Were Watching God.*

Hurston, Zora Neale, 57, 59, 60, 63, 70
writings of, 62–63, 65

I

I Know Why the Caged Bird Sings (Angelou), 50, 84–85, 87, 97
Ice-T, 96
Incidents in the Life of a Slave Girl (Jacobs), 34
Invisible Man (Ellison), 75

J

Jacobs, Harriet, 34
John tales, 13
Johnson, Charles S., 53–57, 55, 65
Johnson, James Weldon, 44–46, 45, 53
Jones, LeRoi. *See* Baraka, Imamu Amiri

K

Kane, Big Daddy, 96
Kincaid, Jamaica, 93
Kindred (Butler), 93
King, Martin Luther, Jr., 76, 79, 79

L

Larsen, Nella, 59, 62
Let the Circle Be Unbroken (Taylor), 92

"Lift Ev'ry Voice and Sing" (James W. Johnson), 44–46, 50
Lindsay, Vachel, 61
LL Cool J, 96
Locke, Alain, 57

M

Malcolm X, 79, 79
Marshall, Paule, 80
M.C. Higgins, the Great (Hamilton), 92
McKay, Claude, 59, 60, 62, 70, 93
Morrison, Toni, 88, 90, 90–91
Mosley, Walter, 93
Myers, Walter Dean, 92

N

Narrative of the Life of Frederick Douglass, an American Slave (Douglass), 32–33, 35
National Urban League, 53
Native Son (Wright), 70, 72, 75

O

Of Love and Dust (Gaines), 80
"On the Pulse of Morning" (Angelou), 84
Opportunity (magazine), 53–54, 61
Oral tradition, 11, 13

P

Passing (Larsen), 62

Pennington, James, 28

Petry, Ann, *69, 70*

The Piano Lesson (Wilson), 91

Precious (film), 93

Prince, Lucy Terry, 20–21

Push (Sapphire), 93

R

Race/racism, as theme of black
   literature
   during civil rights movement, 70,
      76–78, 80
   in current literature, 91, 93
   during Harlem Renaissance, 60,
      62–63, 65

A Raisin in the Sun (Hansberry), 80

Randall, Alice, 96

Rap, 96

"The Revolution Will Not Be
   Televised" (Scott-Heren), 95

Robeson, Paul, 66

Roll of Thunder, Hear My Cry
   (Taylor), 92

Roots (Haley), 81

Roper, Moses, 26

*Running a Thousand Miles for
   Freedom* (Craft and Craft), 31

S

Sapphire, 91, 93

Scorpions (Myers), 92

Scott-Heron, Gil, 95

Seraph on the Suwanee (Hurston),
   70

Shange, Ntozake, 95

Slave narratives, 25–33

"The Slave Mother" (Harper), 24

Slavery, 9
   factors in abolition of, 35–36
   as focus of early black writers,
      22–23
   folk stories reflecting, 13, 15

Smith, Bessie, 66

Songs, 15–17

The Souls of Black Folks (DuBois), *49,*
   49–50

Spirituals, 15–17

T

Taylor, Mildred, 92
   *Life of Olaudah Equiano or Gustavus
      Vassa the African* (Equiano),
      29–31
   Their Eye's Were Watching God
      (Hurston), 60, 66

Till, Emmett, 78

Toomer, Jean, 56

Tuskegee Institute, *46, 47*

U

Up from Slavery (Booker T.
   Washington), 40, 48

V

Van Doren, Carl, 56

Vassa, Gustavus. *See* Equiano, Olaudah

W

Walker, Alice, 87–88

Walker, David, 23

Wallace, George, 76

Washington, Booker T., 40, *40*, 46–48, 51

Washington, George, 20

Waters, Ethel, 66

The Watsons Go to Birmingham, 1963 (Curtis), 92

"We Wear the Mask" (Dunbar), 41–42

Wheatley, Phillis, 7, *7*, 18–20, 19, *19*, 93

"When a Woman Blue" (song), 43

"When Malinday Sings" (Dunbar), 41

Whitfield, James M., 30

will.i.am, 96

Wilson, August, 91

Winans, CeCe, 96

Wright, Richard, 66, 70–72, *71*, 91

Y

Yerby, Frank, 70

Picture Credits

Cover: © Bettmann/Corbis

AP Images, 55, 71, 86

AP Images/David Bookstaver, 90

AP Images/Jacob Harris, 69

Arthur P. Bedou/Robert Abbott Sengstacke/Getty Images, 46

© Bettmann/Corbis, 54, 58, 74, 77, 79, 81

The Bridgeman Art Library/Getty Images, 16

© Corbis, 45, 61, 63, 64

© Leif Skoogfors/Corbis, 85

The Library of Congress, 14, 29, 40, 42, 49

© Louie Psihoyos/Corbis, 34

Malcolm Ali/WireImage/Getty Images, 94

Michael Ochs Archives/Getty Images, 43

MPI/Getty Images, 7

Ms. Virginia (Esther) Hamilton, 92

© North Wind Picture Archives/Alamy, 10, 12, 19, 27, 33

Peter Kramer/Getty Images, 89

Popperfoto/Getty Images, 73

Roadell Hickman/The Plain Dealer/ Landov, 38

About the Author

Stephen Currie is a writer whose publications include many books on African American history and culture. His works for Lucent include *African American Folklore, The African American Religious Experience*, and a number of books on slavery and civil rights, among many others. Currie grew up in Chicago, about half a mile from the high school attended by former Illinois poet laureate Gwendolyn Brooks, and lives now in New York State, where he enjoys kayaking, reading, and hiking.